RUGBY LEA
JOURNAL
ANNUAL
2007

RUGBY LEAGUE JOURNAL
PUBLISHING

First published in Great Britain in 2006 by
Rugby League Journal Publishing
P.O.Box 22, Egremont, Cumbria, CA23 3WA

ISBN 0-9548355-2-2
ISBN 13: 9780954835521

Edited and designed by Harry Edgar

Sales and Marketing by Ruth Edgar

Printed by Printexpress (Cumbria) Limited

Front cover pictures:
Kevin Ward - playing for Great Britain against Rest of the World in 1988.
Mal Meninga and Shaun Edwards in the 1992 Ashes series.
Phil Clarke and Denis Betts playing for England in the 1995 World Cup.

RUGBY LEAGUE JOURNAL
PUBLISHING

P.O. Box 22, Egremont, Cumbria, CA23 3WA
E-Mail: rugbyleague.journal@virgin.net   Telephone: 01946 814249
www.rugbyleaguejournal.net

CONTENTS

The Ashes - for so long the symbol of international Rugby League supremacy. In this picture being presented to Great Britain's captain Willie Horne of Barrow after victory over Australia in the 1952 series.

Our thanks to all the photographers whose skills have provided so many fine images in this book. Many of them no longer with us, and with so many old pictures from private collections it is often difficult to ascertain their origins., thus there has been no intention to breach anybody's copyright. Special thanks to photographers: Eddie Whitham, who has unearthed some wonderful pictures from his archives; Andrew Varley, talented chief photographer of the former "Open Rugby" magazine and Mike McKenzie. Thanks also to friends Andy Wheelwright, Sam Coulter and Ron Bailey for all their help in providing photographs.

This book is dedicated to all the people who shaped the great events of Rugby League's wonderful history - especially in 2007, Albert Henry Baskerville, as we celebrate the 100th Anniversary of his visit with the pioneering team from New Zealand which gave life to the international game.

Introduction

Welcome to the third Annual to be produced by *"Rugby League Journal,"* which we describe as being for fans who don't want to forget the game they used to know. As we wallow unashamedly in another huge selection of nostalgia and memorabilia, we hope readers will enjoy their memories of the Rugby League players, teams and famous events of the past.

In the year 2007, Rugby League will celebrate the 100th anniversary of its birth as a true international sport which came as a result of the pioneering tour by Albert Henry Baskerville and his New Zealand team who have gone down in history as the "All Golds." What brave men they must have been to undertake such a risky adventure back in 1907, but what a great legacy they created. As an acknowledgment of that 100th anniversary, in this Annual we present a section on the international game in its various guises which provides just a quick glimpse of its story - involving the major Test playing nations: Australia, Great Britain, New Zealand and France (the four founders of the World Cup.)

We also present a page of nostalgia on each of the old professional clubs you grew up with, including Bramley (next year we'll have to have Liverpool City and Huyton.) On each of these pages you will find a quick quiz question about each particular club, so you can test the knowledge of the Rugby League expert in your immediate neighbourhood - and see the answers printed on page 104.

In the year in which a professional club was launched again in Wales, we pay tribute to the contribution made over the years by the Welsh to Rugby League as well as praising the efforts of the new Celtic Crusaders.

This Annual, like our quarterly *"Journal,"* is produced on behalf of people who enjoy remembering Rugby League in years gone by, when it was a very different game to the one we see today. But it is fascinating to think what those famous players of the past and the pioneers like Baskerville would make of the modern game in 2006. Certainly they would see in England at the top level of the professional game a very vibrant club competition, driven by the publicity given, and huge funds invested, by that relatively new phenomena - satellite television.

Their product, the Super League, continues to attract increasing attendances with the leading clubs continuing to promote themselves very successfully. And, as the climax of their season, the draw of the newly expanded Old Trafford has helped build the Grand Final into a hugely popular event - this year attended by a new record crowd of 72,582. In that Grand Final, St.Helens took the title, making them by some enormous distance the team of the year in 2006. That wrapped up a Cup and League double for the Saints in a Super League season which had seen a levelling out of standards. St.Helens were way ahead of the field until Hull emerged as genuine contenders, but elsewhere the competition was more unpredictable than ever before. At last the Super League cartel of the so-called "big four" appears to have been broken with Hull following up their 2005 Challenge Cup win with a first Grand Final appearance. Just as joyous was a first Challenge Cup Final in 44 years for Huddersfield.

Whilst St.Helens continued to reign supreme, both Leeds and Bradford did not look as all-conquering as in previous years, and Wigan spent much of 2006 in a battle  against relegation which went a long way in creating the drama and excitement which all successful sporting competitions need. Wigan added to that by sacking their coach mid-season and replacing him with the current Great Britain coach Brian Noble - then they broke the transfer-fee record by signing Stuart Fielden *(pictured)* from Bradford. In an era when transfer-fees are largely a thing of the past, this was another reminder of days gone by and that in Rugby League, despite all its changes, there rarely is anything really new under the sun.

The big success stories of 2006 included the rise of Salford. As one who has always had a soft spot for the Red Devils for historical reasons, it was good to see them do so well. Salford see their future hopes linked to the building of a new stadium, and with them will go Rugby League's hopes of re-establishing the major presence it once had around the city of Manchester. For another city on the opposite side of the country, 2006 was a year of great achievement as both Hull and Hull Kingston Rovers were on the rise. Hull in the Grand Final, and Hull K.R. the National League One champions and promoted to Super League.

We don't claim that the presence of the *"Rugby League Journal"* over the past four years has influenced this, but it is very pleasing to see so many people now acknowledging the past and some clubs now honouring their own histories after the early years of Super League seemed to ride roughshod over the game's heritage. Several - notably Bradford and Warrington - have heritage projects on the go, whilst St.Helens took the wonderful initiative of inviting Tom Van Vollenhoven to lead them out at the 2006 Challenge Cup Final after presenting the Saints players with their jerseys. The major challenge facing the Rugby League's leaders now is to find the right way to maintain the game at the level below Super League and thus preserve it in many of its heartlands which are now feeling so alienated from the mainstream. These are the areas which still pack buses with fans going the Super League Grand Finals and Challenge Cup Finals, but whose local clubs are being left to wither. And they all played major parts in the game we used to know, and don't want to forget.

Harry Edgar (Editor)

HOW THEY FINISHED

FINAL LEAGUE TABLES

2006

SUPER LEAGUE

	P	W	D	L	For	Ag	Diff	Pts
St. Helens	28	24	0	4	939	430	509	48
Hull	28	20	0	8	720	578	142	40
Leeds	28	19	0	9	869	543	326	38
Bradford**	28	16	2	10	802	568	234	32
Salford	28	13	0	15	600	539	61	26
Warrington	28	13	0	15	743	721	22	26
Harlequins	28	11	1	16	556	823	-267	23
Wigan**	28	12	0	16	644	715	-71	22
Huddersfield	28	11	0	17	609	753	-144	22
Wakefield Trin.	28	10	0	18	591	717	-126	20
Castleford	28	9	1	18	575	968	-393	19
Catalans	28	8	0	20	601	894	-293	16

*(** 2 points deducted for salary cap breaches in 2005)*

NATIONAL LEAGUE ONE

	P	W	D	L	For	Ag	Diff	Pts
Hull K.R.	18	16	0	2	705	338	367	32
Widnes	18	14	0	4	729	449	280	28
Leigh	18	13	0	5	549	334	215	26
Whitehaven	18	12	1	5	516	408	108	25
Rochdale	18	8	0	10	462	435	27	16
Batley	18	8	0	10	393	467	-74	16
Halifax	18	7	0	11	461	508	-47	14
Doncaster	18	6	1	11	458	533	-75	13
York	18	5	0	13	476	533	-77	10
Oldham	18	0	0	18	220	944	-724	0

NATIONAL LEAGUE TWO

	P	W	D	L	For	Ag	Diff	Pts
Dewsbury	22	19	0	3	693	354	339	38
Sheffield	22	18	0	4	808	390	418	36
Celtic Crus.	22	14	1	7	730	387	343	29
Featherstone	22	14	1	7	596	504	92	29
Swinton	22	13	1	8	641	475	166	27
Barrow	22	12	0	10	599	481	118	24
Gateshead	22	11	0	11	547	540	7	22
Workington	22	10	0	12	558	645	-87	20
London Skol.	22	5	1	16	406	776	-370	11
Hunslet	22	4	2	16	411	617	-206	10
Keighley	22	4	1	17	419	736	-317	9
Blackpool	22	4	1	17	350	853	-503	9

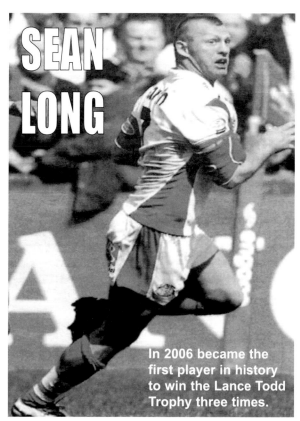

SEAN LONG

In 2006 became the first player in history to win the Lance Todd Trophy three times.

(Picture by courtesy of Andrew Varley.)

DREAM TEAMS

(Official RFL All-Stars merit teams for 2006)

SUPER LEAGUE

1-Paul Wellens (St.Helens); **2-Justin Murphy** (Catalans), **3-Jamie Lyon** (St.Helens), **4-Kirk Yeaman** (Hull), **5-David Hodgson** (Salford); **6-Danny McGuire** (Leeds), **7-Sean Long** (St.Helens); **8-Stuart Fielden** (Wigan & Bradford), **9-Keiron Cunningham** (St.Helens), **10-Danny Nutley** (Castleford), **11-Gareth Ellis** (Leeds), **12-Jon Wilkin** (St.Helens), **13-Kevin Sinfield** (Leeds).

NATIONAL LEAGUE ONE

1-Ben Cockayne (Hull K.R.); **2-Peter Fox** (York), **3-Danny Halliwell** (Leigh), **Jon Goddard** (Hull K.R.), **Byron Ford** (Hull K.R.); **6-Dennis Moran** (Widnes), **7-James Webster** (Hull K.R.); **8-Steve Trindall** (Whitehaven), **9-Mark Smith** (Widnes), **10-David Tangata-Toa** (Hull K.R.), **11-Jason Golden** (York), **12-James Taylor** (Leigh), **13-Bob Beswick** (Widnes).

NATIONAL LEAGUE TWO

1-Tony Duggan (Celtic Crusaders); **2-Bryn Powell** (Dewsbury), **3-Chris Hall** (Dewsbury), **4-Liam Harrison** (Barrow), **5-Marlon Billy** (Swinton); **6-Brendon Lindsay** (Sheffield Eagles), **7-Jace Van Dijk** (Celtic Crusaders); **8-Frank Watene** (Dewsbury), **9-Richard Chapman** (Dewsbury), **10-Stuart Dickens** (Featherstone), **11-Warren Jowitt** (Dewsbury), **12-Brett McDermott** (Barrow), **13-Martin Moana** (Swinton).

Lee Briers the entertainer

LEE Briers is the *Rugby League Journal* choice as Super League's player-of-the-year for 2006. The Warrington captain once again showed all the instinctive ball skills, both with hand and foot, which were a reminder of days gone by when most clubs in the Rugby League had their own favourite stand-off with the creative skills to set up their attacks and entertain the crowds.

Briers did all those things, coming up regularly with vital "forty-twenty" kicks and the important drop-goal when it was most

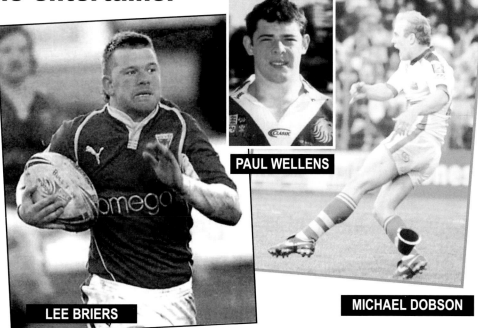

LEE BRIERS

PAUL WELLENS

MICHAEL DOBSON

Picture by courtesy of Andrew Varley.

needed. He may not be the biggest, fastest or strongest player in the League, and he won't top all those statistics charts that seem to dominate the thinking of so many people now in Super League - but ask the neutral fans who was the best footballer around and Lee Briers would be the man. Warrington depended on him to make things happen and no individual was more important to the performance of the whole team than Lee.

Our other top two players are **Paul Wellens** of St.Helens and **Paul Cooke** of Hull. Wellens was a model of consistency for Saints, fearless in defence and a vital part of the attack coming into the line with pace and power. An exemplary player in a brilliant team. Cooke, meanwhile, has many of the same abilities as Lee Briers, with kicking and handling skills to match, but is bigger and more powerful and now plays in the loose-forward position. Hull played some great football and Cooke was at the hub of it all.

Our young player-of-the-year in Super League is 19-years-old **Michael Dobson,** a teenager who had an immense impact on the whole Super League competition in 2006. First, he was rushed to Europe to fill the golden boots of Stacey Jones and hold the new Catalans team together - then he faced the even bigger challenge of providing Wigan with the creative guidance they so desperately needed to turn their season around. More than any other individual, Dobson was the key to Wigan avoiding relegation and they should be forever

grateful to the young bloke for that.

In National One our top players were **James Webster** of Hull K.R. and **Gary Broadbent** of Whitehaven. The little scrum-half Webster was vital in making the Champion Robins team tick - without him they were nothing like as impressive. Broadbent had other consistently influential players around him at Whitehaven in 2006 in Leroy Joe and Carl Rudd, but - just like Paul Wellens at Saints - was a model professional and rock-solid full-back.

In National League Two hooker **Richard Chapman** was a key man in the Champion side Dewsbury, Aussie full-back **Tony Duggan** provided the spark for new boys Celtic Crusaders, but none was such an inspiration as **Brett McDermott,** returning to his home club Barrow.

SUPER LEAGUE CENTURY POINTS SCORERS
(Regular season Super League games only)

Player	Team	Tries	Goals	Drops	Total
Jamie Lyon	(St.Helens)	17	124	0	316
Lee Briers	(Warrington)	8	102	7	243
Michael Dobson	(Catalans/Wigan)	9	97	1	221
Paul Deacon	(Bradford)	6	100	0	220
Jamie Rooney	(Wakefield)	14	69	3	197
Kevin Sinfield	(Leeds)	2	90	0	188
Paul Cooke	(Hull)	2	80	2	170
David Hodgson	(Salford)	13	44	0	140
Danny Brough	(Hull/Castleford)	2	56	2	122
Michael De Vere	(Huddersfield)	5	49	0	118
Rob Burrow	(Leeds)	12	34	0	116
Chris Thorman	(Huddersfield)	6	40	0	104
Justin Murphy	(Catalans)	25	0	0	100

SUPER LEAGUE

ST. HELENS - The perfect year for Saints winning everything available to them - the "double" of Challenge Cup and Championship, plus the league leaders' shield. Plus all the game's top individual awards - Man of Steel to Paul Wellens, young player-of-the-year to James Graham, coach-of-the-year in Daniel Anderson, Lance Todd Trophy to Sean Long and Harry Sunderland trophy to Paul Wellens. Hope they've got plenty of silver polish to keep all those trophies shining in the Knowlsey Road cabinet.

Their 26-4 win over Hull in the Grand Final at a packed Old Trafford put the seal on it all for St.Helens who had looked a class above everybody else for most of the year - until they came up against the determined "Airlie Birds" later in the campaign. Runaway leaders of the Super League table, Saints reaped the rewards of having Daniel Anderson at the helm - a fine ambassador for the club and role model for the players, the St.Helens discipline and defensive organisation backed up all their flair and pace in attack as Anderson kept the wheels rolling smoothly.

HULL - A wonderful season for Hull as they backed up last year's Challenge Cup win with their first Super League Grand Final. Their inventive and attractive football, largely orchestrated by the outstanding Paul Cooke, was rewarded with second place as they were the one team to have the measure of St.Helens. They didn't deserve that 26-4 scoreline in the Grand Final. Hull's season turned around after they parted company with John Kear as coach. Richard Swain came back to show he was the best dummy-half organiser in Super League and new coach Peter Sharp came in and got the best out of all the players, who included a whole crop of talented young local Hull boys. A job well done and a bright future ahead for the black and whites.

LEEDS - Most Leeds fans would regard it as a disappointing season although they still managed to finish third, six points ahead of the fourth team Bradford. Injuries hampered them - notably to Richard Mathers and Danny McGuire - and with new players coming in yet to fulfil expectations and others known to be on the way out, it seemed to be a time of upheaval. The

ROB BURROW
Leeds favourite.

Rhinos' previous air of invincibility at Headingley started to look vulnerable, probably not helped by running towards an empty building-site for much of the season, the end product of which was the magnificent new Carnegie Stand opened in September and making grand old Headingley ever better. Leeds were still the best supported club in the British game.

BRADFORD - Another World Club Challenge title at the start of the year, and the Bulls ended the campaign just one game away from another Grand Final in a controversial defeat at Hull after coming through from fourth place. In between, it was an up and down season for Bradford - it said much about the English teams' reliance on far too many overseas players when, for much of the year, the veteran Stanley Gene was the most exciting player at Odsal. But Bradford do have a fine crop of home-bred youngsters coming through the ranks, none better than teenager Sam Burgess and Brett Ferres who

LUKE ROBINSON
Salford star.

established themselves as first-teamers. Talk of financial worries was never far away, but the mid-season upheaval of losing coach Brian Noble and prop Stuart Fielden to Wigan did not stop the Bulls doing well in the play-offs.

SALFORD - A big achievement for Salford to finish fifth and make the Super League play-offs for the first time. The Reds were popular achievers because they played some excellent football all season and were desperately unlucky on several occasions in the face of refereeing controversies not to get more winning points on the board. Salford's strength was that their best players were British players, inexplicably overlooked for international selection. Outstanding performances all year from winger/fullback David Hodgson, scrum-half Luke Robinson and forwards Andy Coley and big Gareth Haggerty..

HENRY FA'AFILI
Warrington wing.

WARRINGTON - A few hiccups along the way, but Warrington did make the top six and proceded to show how good they could be with a great performance and victory at Leeds in the play-offs. That night, as he had been all season, Lee Briers was the key to the Wire's success. His kicking and handling abilities made him the most creative footballer in the Super League, and when he wasn't there (notably in a Challenge Cup defeat at Hull K.R.) Warrington looked a different side. They continued their progress as one of the boom clubs in the game right now, with several full houses at the Halliwell Jones stadium - including a memorable night in the snow against St.Helens - and some more big name signings on the way.

HARLEQUINS - First year under their new name and in new colours for Super League's London club, and things were certainly a lot more enjoyable at the Twickenham Stoop than they had been at Brentford. Crowds were up a bit and a major change came when long-running coach Tony Rea

ROB PURDHAM
Best of British.

moved "upstairs" and Yorkshireman Brian McDermott took over. Performances on the field continued to be the old Broncos mix of good and bad. Aussie skipper Mark McLinden continued to be one of the best attackers in Super League and long-serving Robert Purdham was a constant tower of strength, now having evolved into a second-rower after being a stand-off in his earlier days at Whitehaven. Harlequins added to their box office appeal by signing the mercurial Henry Paul, back from Union.

BRYAN FLETCHER
Valuable forward for Wigan.

WIGAN - What a roller-coaster ride for Wigan in 2006, as for many weeks the very real threat of relegation loomed. To cut the long story short, the cheque book came out again as starting coach Ian Millward rode off into the sunset and another bunch of players found themselves travelling out of the JJB - usually to Widnes. In came the Great Britain coach Brian Noble from Bradford, soon followed by world record transfer-fee man Stuart Fielden, along with the gifted 19-year-old Aussie scrum-half Michael Dobson after his stint with the Catalans ended. They provided the catalyst for Wigan to get out of gaol - and the fans loved it. Big crowds flocked to watch them and Sky Television couldn't get enough of Wigan's "great escape." In the end, they finished eighth - nothing to worry about!

HUDDERSFIELD - A first Challenge Cup Final for Fartown for 44 years was the highspot of a season that followed the same pattern as before - tough, competitive, looking good for the play-offs, only to fall away and be looking over their shoulder at the relegation battle. The Cup Final at Twickenham was a real achievement and it was especially pleasing for chairman Ken Davy to see the claret and gold in a major final. The debut season of Robbie Paul certainly helped Huddersfield on and off the field, whilst hooker Brad Drew was their key player.

WAKEFIELD TRINITY - Phew, this truly *was* the great escape! Trinity looked destined for the drop when they appointed John Kear as coach with six games to go. They needed to win four of those to have a chance of staying up and they did it magnificently - the fight back climaxing in a wonderful night of emotion as an 11,000 capacity crowd packed Belle Vue for the sudden-death showdown with neighbours Castleford. So Wakefield live to fight another season in Super League - their almost total dependence on overseas players in 2006 a depressing sign of the times.

CASTLEFORD - A few weeks from the end of the season it seemed Castleford had confounded all the critics, beaten all the hurdles confronting a newly promoted club, and would be staying up with a total of 19 points compared to the five points of last year's relegated Leigh. Then it all went wrong, culminating in that heart-breaker at Wakefield in their last match of the season. Cas' had a roller-coaster of a year, going from one extreme to the other, which must have left their new coach from Australia, Terry Matterson, feeling bemused. Full-back Michael Platt was outstanding in a year in which Cas' finally said goodby to Brad Davis. Will they bounce back? Castleford have shown before that they can do it.

CATALANS - The new French adventure got off to a great start with an 11,000 crowd and victory over Wigan, providing many feelings of *deja-vu* with the debut of Paris St.Germain a decade ago. They also started without a coach, until Mick Potter arrived from Australia. It was always going to be very tough for French players playing in the modern game that is Super League and all that goes with it, but they stayed determined and finished with 16 points from eight wins. That could have been more had their talisman Stacey Jones not broken his arm and missed a few months. It was a solid debut season in that they made a big impression in their own local area, and added a big attraction for travelling English fans.

SUPER LEAGUE TOP TRIES & GOALS		
(Regular season Super League games only)		
TOP TRY SCORERS		
Justin Murphy	(Catalans)	25
Danny McGuire	(Leeds)	24
Ade Gardner	(St.Helens)	24
Kirk Yeaman	(Hull)	21
Henry Fa'afili	(Warrington)	20
Paul Wellens	(St.Helens)	18
Shontayne Hape	(Bradford)	17
TOP GOAL KICKERS		
Jamie Lyon	(St.Helens)	124
Lee Briers	(Warrington)	102
Paul Deacon	(Bradford)	100
Michael Dobson	(Catalans/Wigan)	97
Kevin Sinfield	(Leeds)	90
Paul Cooke	(Hull)	80
Jamie Rooney	(Wakefield)	69

NATIONAL LEAGUE ONE

CARL RUDD - all class for Whitehaven.

HULL KINGSTON ROVERS - League leaders and Grand Final winners, and with that the coveted promotion to Super League, plus a Challenge Cup semi-final, made it a season of glory for the Robins. All major ambitions achieved for coach Justin Morgan and a famous club out of the top flight since the Super League era began. Rovers had stand-out players in skipper James Webster, young stand-off Scott Murrell, centre Jon Goddard and fast-moving full-back Ben Cockayne.

WIDNES - It ended in disappoinment with their 29-16 loss to Hull K.R. in the Grand Final, which left Widnes feeling pretty down as all their season had been geared towards winning an instant return to Super League. That saw plenty of players in and out at Widnes and a heavy influx of ex-Wigan lads as well as the mighty Barrie McDermott. Hooker Mark Smith was outstanding and big centre Mick Nanyn brought his prolific points scoring ability with him from Whitehaven.

LEIGH - The third of the full-time pro' teams came up short at the end losing at home to Batley in the play-offs - a big shock for their Kiwi coach Tony Benson. The other side of the coin was lifting the Northern Rail Cup, beating Hull K.R. in the final at Blackpool. Led from the front by skipper Paul Rowley, Leigh had emerging young talent in Carl Forber, Scot Grix and James Taylor.

WHITEHAVEN - Finished fourth as the best of the semi-pro clubs and were very close to beating Widnes in the play-offs and going to their third Grand Final in a row. A glut of injuries hit them hard early season, but by the end of it 'Haven were at their best. Superb seasons from the ever reliable Gary Broadbent and Leroy Joe, with Carl Rudd all class; and more top local promise emerging in Scott McAvoy and Graeme Mattinson. An enjoyable first season for new coach Dave Rotheram.

ROCHDALE - Hornets coach Darren Abram could be pleased with his team achieving fifth place and giving some of the top clubs hidings along the way. Much hard work going in off the field to rebuild the Rochdale club commercially. On the field, top performers in full-back Chris Giles, centres Mark McCully and Kevin King and prop Rob Ball.

BATLEY - Confounded pre-season forecasts of a relegation battle by finishing sixth and going into the play-offs where they caused a big upsest winning at Leigh. This helped Batley's Gary Thonrton be named the division's coach-of-the-year. Unearthed a fiery little half-back from Leigh in Jay Duffy and had another consistent season from full-back Craig Lingard, with Michael Wainwright a lively centre.

HALIFAX - A traumatic season climaxed with Halifax going close to being wound up as the problems of the summer game outside Super League took their toll. Former chairman Howard Posner came to the rescue at the eleventh hour with the cash to bail them out. Coach Anthony Farrell was replaced mid-season by Martin Hall as 'Fax finished in seventh place. Scrum-half Joel Penny tried hard to guide them but it was a tough year for the blue and whites.

DONCASTER - Poor results for a club who talk big plans for the future but who finished just one place away from relegation and struggled to get a 1,000 crowd. Everything seemed to centre around Graham Holroyd on the field along with Peter Green.

YORK - Disappointment of immediate relegation for newly promoted York, but just one more win against Doncaster and York would have stayed up. Still a vibrant club, the men from the Minster City are well supported. Winger Peter Fox was one the best in the division.

OLDHAM - Long before the end of the season, everybody was feeling sorry for Oldham. With all finances directed to paying off tax debts, Oldham struggled to stay competitive in a very competitive league - finishing as only the fourth team in R.L. history to go a whole campaign without winning a single point. In last place and relegated was not what new coach Steve Deakin would want on his C.V.

LEADING SCORERS
(In National League regular season games)

TOP TRY SCORERS

Mick Nanyn	(Widnes)	23
Dennis Moran	(Widnes)	18
Danny Halliwell	(Leigh)	18
Craig Lingard	(Batley)	16
Ben Cockayne	(Hull K.R.)	16
Chris Giles	(Rochdale)	16
Mark Smith	(Widnes)	15
Shad Royston	(Doncaster)	14
Lee Greenwood	(Leigh)	13
Craig Calvert	(Whitehaven)	13
Peter Fox	(York)	13
James Webster	(Hull K.R.)	13
Joel Penny	(Halifax)	13

TOP GOAL KICKERS

Mick Nanyn	(Widnes)	105
Carl Rudd	(Whitehaven)	71
Graham Holroyd	(Doncaster)	66(2)
Gareth Morton	(Hull K.R.)	49
Kevin King	(Rochdale)	44
James Haley	(Halifax)	44
Damien Couturier	(Hull K.R.)	38
Steve Jones	(Batley)	32
Mark McCully	(Rochdale)	29
Julian O'Neill	(Leigh)	28(1)

(Drop-goals included in totals)

CENTURY POINTS SCORERS

Mick Nanyn	(Widnes)	302
Carl Rudd	(Whitehaven)	150
Graham Holroyd	(Doncaster)	146
Gareth Morton	(Hull K.R.)	126
James Haley	(Halifax)	120
Kevin King	(Rochdale)	104

NATIONAL LEAGUE TWO

WAISALE SOVATABUA -
Sheffield Wembley survivor.

CRESTA - bags
of enthusiasm.

DEWSBURY - Champions and promoted - that's as good as it could get for Dewsbury in a great season for a club that has rebuilt itself from the brink of disaster a couple of years ago. Their team was packed with experience with the likes of Francis Maloney, Kevin Crouthers, Warren Jowitt, Richard Chapman, Darren Rogers combining well with young local talent. A job well done by coach Andy Kelly and chairman Mark Sawyer.

SHEFFIELD - Promotion at last for the Eagles with their fine victory over Swinton in the play-off Grand Final, after finishing in second place behind Dewsbury. Sheffield's top performers included full-back Jonny Woodcock, captain and back-rower Andy Smith, experienced half-back Gavin Brown and the two big props Jack Howieson and Mitchell Stringer. The popular Eagles were always ready to give new talent a chance.

CELTIC CRUSADERS - A very impressive debut season by the team from South Wales, achieving third place and just an extra-time drop-goal away from appearing in the play-off Grand Final. Their performances deserved to see much bigger crowds in Bridgend. A strong Aussie influence with stars in full-back Tony Duggan and scrum-half Jace Van Dijk.

FEATHERSTONE - No instant return to Division One for Rovers. Fourth place and knocked out at home in the play-offs by Swinton. Steve Dickens continued a fine Featherstone tradition of goal-kicking forwards, and there were good shows by forwards Steve Dooler and full-back Nathan Larvin.

SWINTON - Optimism at the end of the season for Swinton fans - a great run in the play-offs all the way to the Grand Final and news of a site for a planned home of their own close to the old Station Road. Long-serving full-back Wayne English was as good as ever for the Lions with Lee Marsh another star.

BARROW - A great effort from all concerned at Craven Park to keep the club going and achieve a play-off place after the genuine fears during the pre-season that Barrow Rugby could disappear. The enthusiasm brought by new coach, local boy Paul "Cresta" Crarey, was a key factor. Brett McDermott was an inspired signing providing leadership for the youngsters, among whom centre Liam Harrison showed great promise.

GATESHEAD - Another season of much improved results on the field, but another year of struggle to draw a crowd for Gateshead. People put in so much hard work and personal investment to keep the club going, but they must think that in the world of Rugby League little goes in their favour. Aussie Wade Liddell was a star performer and there was the usual 100% contribution from locals Kevin Neighbour and Neil Thorman.

WORKINGTON - Big disappointment for Town who had expected such big things in 2006. Not even a play-off place in a year of inconsistency. The positives included the promise of the teenage Lunt brothers and Liam Campbell - and the never-say-die effort of Garry Purdham.

LONDON SKOLARS - Full of optimism as always, the Skolars enjoyed five wins under new coach Latham Tawhai. Got the community club-of-the-year for all their hard work and a biggest ever 1,000-plus crowd for an eve of Cup Final event.

HUNSLET - Disappointed to finish third bottom, it was a tough baptism for new player-coach Mark Cass. Hunslet's best included hooker Darren Robinson and Mark Sibson.

KEIGHLEY - Still haven't recovered from their promotion and instant relegation two years ago. Even the experience of Barry Eaton couldn't get some more wins for Keighley.

BLACKPOOL - Bottom on points difference from Keighley it was a poor season for Blackpool - but they'll be back next year playing at Fylde R.U.

LEADING SCORERS
(In National League regular season games)

TOP TRY SCORERS

Tony Duggan	(Celtic Crus.)	27
James Ford	(Sheffield)	19
Andy Saywell	(Swinton)	18
James Nixon	(Barrow)	18
Shaun Lunt	(Workington)	17
Eric Andrews	(Blackpool)	16
Wade Liddell	(Gateshead)	16
Wayne McHugh	(Featherstone)	16
Michael Ryan	(Celtic Crus.)	15
Richard Chapman	(Dewsbury)	15

TOP GOAL KICKERS

Darren Holt	(Barrow)	82(3)
Stuart Dickens	(Featherstone)	81
Jonny Woodcock	(Sheffield)	69
Damien Quinn	(Celtic Crus.)	65
Wade Liddell	(Gateshead)	63
Barry Eaton	(Keighley)	63
Francis Maloney	(Dewsbury)	53(2)
Stephen Kirkbride	(Workington)	49(1)
Liam Finn	(Dewsbury)	42
Lee Marsh	(Swinton)	41(1)
(Drop goals included in totals)		

CENTURY POINTS SCORERS

Wade Liddell	(Gateshead)	200
Stuart Dickens	(Featherstone)	182
Jonny Woodcock	(Sheffield)	182
Damien Quinn	(Celtic Crus.)	178
Darren Holt	(Barrow)	173
Barry Eaton	(Keighley)	146
Liam Finn	(Dewsbury)	136
Francis Maloney	(Dewsbury)	120
Tony Duggan	(Celtic Crus.)	108
Eric Andrews	(Blackpool)	106
Shaun Lunt	(Workington)	106

Kevin Ward

A great British forward

We pay tribute to the front-cover star of this year's *"Rugby League Journal Annual"* - Kevin Ward - a great British forward of the modern era who gave fine service to both Castleford and St.Helens as well as being a dominating figure on the international scene.

KEVIN Ward was a forward respected throughout the Rugby League world and was a particular favourite at the Castleford and St.Helens clubs he served so well. A mighty prop, he won the respect of the Aussies in Test football and then when he went to play for Manly in the Winfield Cup.

Ward played in the modern era, but for forwards especially it was a very different game to the one we see today. Big men like Kevin would still play a full 80 minutes, still push at the scrums, and still do all the heavy work up front. And, of course, fellows like Kevin Ward would still have to do a full week's work (in his case hard labour on a building site) before they got to play their football. Yet in the 1980s it was an era when the rules of the game had evolved to make Rugby League a great spectacle thanks largely to the influence of the 1982 Kangaroos. We had six-tackles and the turnover rule, but the hard yards still had to be made and there was no unlimited interchange as Ward led the British pack in three Ashes series against giant forward opponents like Paul Sironen, Steve Roach, Noel Cleal and Glenn Lazarus.

The picture *(above)* shows Kevin working a special runaround move with Andy Gregory which he perfected on the 1988 Lions tour. That was a year after Manly had flown him back to Sydney to play in their Grand Final in which he gave an outstanding performance. Sadly, Ward's career was cut short by a very serious leg injury whilst playing for St.Helens.

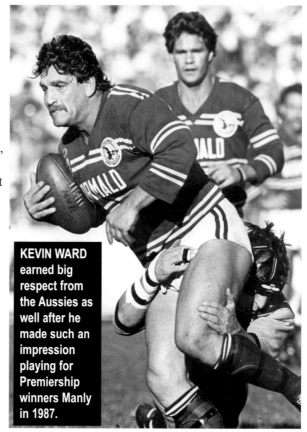

KEVIN WARD earned big respect from the Aussies as well after he made such an impression playing for Premiership winners Manly in 1987.

SAINTS LOVE SILVERWARE

Challenge Cups and Super League titles - they've had them aplenty over the last decade at St.Helens. For much of the modern era, Saints have been known as the entertainers of the Rugby League, and they've also had the taste for silver.
(Right) Bobbie Goulding was the proud Saints captain who lifted the very first Super League title in 1996, whilst *(above)* Tommy Martyn took the Lance Todd Trophy as St.Helens won the Challenge Cup at Wembley in 1997.

Souvenir of the

NEW ZEALAND

RUGBY

FOOTBALL TEAM

AKE AKE KIA KAHA!!

1907-8

OFFICIAL SOUVENIR

Published by the New Zealand Rugby Football Team
of the 1907-8 Tour.

2007 marks the 100-year anniversary of the birth of international Rugby League as the game celebrates the arrival on British shores (via Australia) in 1907 of A. H. Baskerville's New Zealand team - the All Blacks who have gone down in sporting legend as the "All Golds."

True Pioneers

The Pioneers of international Rugby League - the 1907 All Golds.
Left to right:
Back row: W.Trevarthen, H.R.Wright *(captain),* W.Johnston, T.Cross, A.Lile, C.J.Pearce, D.G.Fraser.
Third row: H.F.Rowe, G.W. Smith *(vice-captain),* W.Mackrell, E.Wrigley, J.A.Lavery, C.A.Byrne, D.Gilchrist, E.L.Watkins, W.T.Tyler.
Second row: R.J.Wynyard, C.Dunning, L.B.Todd, D.McGregor, Mr. H.J.Palmer *(manager),* H.S.Turtill, J.C.Gleeson *(treasurer),* W.T.Wynyard.
Front row: A. Callum, H.Tyne, A.H.Baskerville *(secretary),* H.H.Messenger, A.F.Kelly.

THE men pictured on the faded old photograph *(above)* could hardly have imagined what their legacy would be 100 years on from the moment they posed together in the all black football uniforms of New Zealand.

As they set sail out of Auckland in August 1907, first for Australia *en route* to Mother England, none could have guessed that a century later they would be remembered with such reverence and admiration. Because these were the men who created international Rugby League - not only did they give birth to Test football, they started the game in New Zealand, provided the catalyst for its launch in Australia, and effectively cemented the very existence of the game in its birthplace, England.

In the autumn of 2007, the Rugby Football League will celebrate the 100th Anniversary of the birth of the international game by inviting New Zealand to send another touring team to British shores, to play a Test series against England and the re-enactment of a "Northern Union versus All Golds" match at Headingley. This will be a birthday tribute to the game between the two teams so named which is in the game's official records as its first *bona-fide* Test match and was played at the same venue in Leeds on 18th January 1908 and won by the "British" side 14-6. It should be noted that it was not the very first international under the auspices of the Northern Union as, a couple of weeks earlier, on New Year's Day 1908, the New Zealanders had played against Wales in Aberdare.

That the pioneering tour of

(Above) A scene from the All Golds tour as leading referee of the time Mr. J.H.Smith, second from the left with the watch chain, helped give the tourists instruction in Northern Union rules - alongside him leading players J.C.Gleeson, "Dally" Messenger, "Bumper" Wright (the New Zealand captain in the hat) and George Smith.

1907-08 took place was largely due to the incredible enthusiasm, determination and organising ability of a young postal worker from Wellington, New Zealand, named Albert Henry Baskerville. He was only 24-years-of-age when he began communicating (by post) with officials of the Northern Union in England with a view to bringing a group of players to Britain to play against their teams.

Baskerville and his players rode the gauntlet of fierce opposition from the New Zealand Rugby Union and, because they were deemed to be professionals, they were taunted with the name "All Golds" rather than allowed to be "All Blacks." Yet each player had to contribute in advance between £50 and £100 apiece, which for a working-class man in 1907 would be the best part of a year's salary. Their courage was rewarded when the tour made a handsome profit. In total, the New Zealanders (who whilst in Australia had enlisted the services of the top Aussie player "Dally" Messenger) played 35 games; winning 19, drawing two and losing 14.

The name "All Golds" has come to be regarded as a badge of honour for the men who allowed the Northen Union to expand its horizons to become an international sport. Tragically, Baskerville died from pneumonia in Australia on the way home from the tour, but this young man's place in history is assured as the pioneer of the international game.

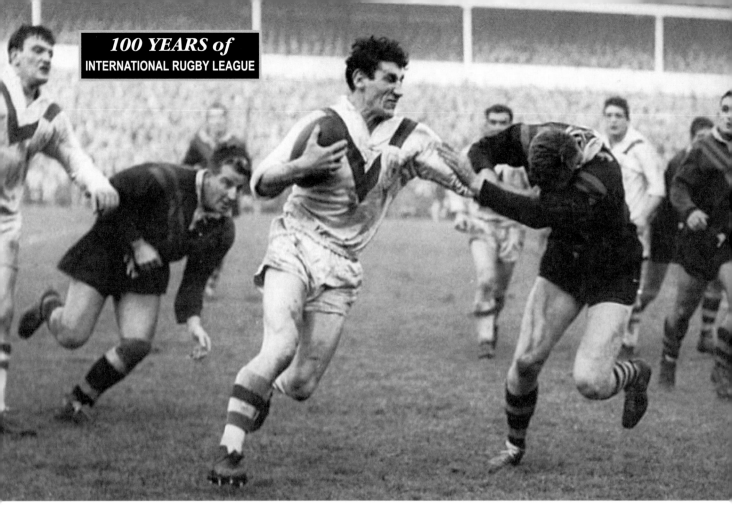

The Battle for the Ashes

THE Battle for the Ashes between the British and the Australians was, for most of international Rugby League's first 100 years, the rock on which the game was built. So much of the game's legends and folklore, its tales of great deeds, heroics and heartbreaks, have been wrapped up in the history of the Ashes and with it, of course, the wider history of the great tours by the Lions and the Kangaroos.

The photograph *(above)* encapsulates so much of that Ashes story. Firstly because it pictures the mighty Vince Karalius on the charge against the Aussies. Vince, whose repuation was built on the rip-roaring 1958 Lions tour and who will be forever remembered by the nickname the Australians bestowed on him as a result - *"The Wild Bull of the Pampas."* His role in the story of the Ashes was written in stone from the moment he played in his first Test against Australia - the epic Brisbane match in 1958 in which his skipper Alan Prescott played the whole game with a broken arm.

No substitutes allowed then and none in the match *(above)* which proved to be the last time Karalius played in a Test for Great Britain. This was the second Test of the 1963 series played at Station Road, Swinton and Great Britain, with captain Eric Ashton and stand-off Frank Myler both injured early in the first-half, played most of

the game with only eleven men and were thrashed 50 points to 12. It remains a special day circled brightly in the history of Australian Rugby League, not just for the sheer quality of the performance put on by a team containing so many of their finest ever players (names like Gasnier, Langlands, Irvine, Thornett, Walsh and Raper among them) but moreso because it was the day they won the Ashes on British soil for the fist time in over fifty years.

Australia's only previous series win here had been way back in 1911-12 when Chris McKivat's second Kangaroos took the prize that would prove so elusive for their fellow countrymen for much of the next half century.

The so-called "Swinton massacre" of 1963 was also a very significant milestone for the British - the day we lost the Ashes on home soil never to win them again on our own turf. In the ensuing 43 years, only Great Britain's win on the 1970 Lions tour has broken Australia's stranglehold on the Ashes and every single Kangaroo touring team has gone home from England with the trophy.

Another part of the Ashes story is the grounds on which the Test matches were played, the famous stadiums which provided the stage for history to be unfolded upon. Whilst in Australia the Sydney Cricket Ground and the various Brisbane venues were the places all British followers came to learn about, at home in England, Station Road at

The moment which announced the arrival of one of the great names in the history of Ashes football - as Australian centre Reg Gasnier touches down for one of his hat-trick of tries in the opening Test of the 1959 series at Station Road, Swinton. Billy Boston is the British defender left in his wake - this was Gasnier's very first match against Great Britain and what a debut!

Swinton was the most revered of all Ashes venues - moreso than others like Headingley, Odsal, or even Wembley. Station Road, situated in the northern suburbs of the city of Manchester, had seen a long list of famous Ashes moments beginning with, perhaps, its most controversial of all in the very first Test match played there in January 1930. That was the match which finished as a nil-nil draw after Australia's scrum-half Joe "Chimpy" Busch had a try disallowed in the corner just two minutes from full-time. History has come to tell us that the Aussies were robbed that day - of victory and the Ashes - by a linesman's flag. It would not be the last time decisions by officials were to cause controversy in the drama of the Ashes.

Swinton was also the venue when Reg Gasnier, one of the Australian "immortals," made his sensational entry to the arena of Ashes football with a hat-trick of tries. That was in 1959 on the first of three full

(Above) Last time Great Britain won the Ashes - as captain Frank Myler is carried aloft with the trophy around Sydney Cricket Ground in 1970 by the jubilant Dennis Hartley and Cliff Watson with a smiling Tony Fisher looking on.

Kangaroo tours which Gasnier made to Europe as his name became the benchmark for quality in Rugby League. Four years after Gasnier's debut he was back at Station Road for the infamous "massacre" of 1963, and he looked on injured from the sidelines as the captain-coach of the 1967 Australian team which clinched the Ashes again, in arctic conditions of a frozen pitch and snow blizzards.

Alas, Station Road is no more and, for the time being, so are the Ashes. Last contested in 2003 in England - and not in Australia since 1992 - and with no immediate plan to revive them now that the Tri-Nations series has been introduced as the pinnacle of international Rugby League. The tradition was born way back in December 1908 when the very first Anglo-Australian Test match was played at the Park Royal stadium in London. Britain's 30 year dominance before 1950 has been replaced by Australia's dominance since 1970. Will the game's greatest tradition ever be revived for future generations?

Action from the historic first World Cup Final in Paris in 1954 - as Great Britain forward Don Robinson evades the diving tackle of French prop Francois Rinaldi with John Thorley in support.*(Inset)* British captain Dave Valentine becomes the first man to receive the World Cup with, alongside him, Frenchman Paul Barriere, very much the founding father of the tournament.

The World Cup show

THROUGHOUT its history Rugby League has been an innovator, leading the way for other sports to follow - and one of its proudest achievements should have been its establishment of a World Cup. Alas, alongside its enthusiasm for innovation, only Rugby League could show the ability to screw up a good thing as much as it has, on numerous occasions, since the pioneering inaugural World Cup tournament was staged so successfully in France way back in 1954.

Yet, despite a constant flow of scepticism from within the sport for over half a century, the Rugby League World Cup has managed to establish record crowds for the international game in three of the game's four major countries - but now the League game has to stand back and watch the way other sports have adopted their idea and made it work for them.

It wasn't always that way. The first World Cup in 1954, although very much a product of French initiative and the vision of the young president of the French Rugby League, Paul Barriere, provided a wonderful opportunity for the game in Britain. The winning performances of the Great Britain team, heroically led by Scotsman Dave Valentine, was one thing. The fact that the thrilling Final against France at the Parc des Princes was televised live from Paris into the U.K. via the then fledgling "Eurovision Link" (or "Continental Exhange" as it was referred to in 1954) was something else.

Remember, in 1954 the football World Cup had yet to make

ALL THE WORLD CUP TOURNAMENTS

1954 - Staged in France
Winners: GREAT BRITAIN. Runners-up: FRANCE.

1957 - Staged in Australia
Winners: AUSTRALIA. Runners-up: GREAT BRITAIN.

1960 - Staged in England
Winners: GREAT BRITAIN. Runners-up: AUSTRALIA.

1968 - Staged in Australia and New Zealand
Winners: AUSTRALIA. Runners-up: FRANCE

1970 - Staged in England
Winners: AUSTRALIA. Runners-up: GREAT BRITAIN

1972 - Staged in France
Winners: GREAT BRITAIN. Runners-up: AUSTRALIA.

1975 - Staged Worldwide
Winners: AUSTRALIA. Runners-up: ENGLAND.

1977 - Staged in Australia and New Zealand
Winners: AUSTRALIA. Runners-up: GREAT BRITAIN.

1985-88 - Staged Worldwide
Winners: AUSTRALIA. Runners-up: NEW ZEALAND.

1989-92 - Staged Worldwide
Winners: AUSTRALIA. Runners-up: GREAT BRITAIN.

1995 - Staged in England and Wales
Winners: AUSTRALIA. Runners-up: ENGLAND.

2000 - Staged in the British Isles and France
Winners: AUSTRALIA. Runers-up: NEW ZEALAND.

England staged the World Cup for the first time in 1960 and Great Britain beat all the other nations to take the trophy - this action *(above)* is from the Great Britain versus New Zealand match at Odsal Stadium and shows Frank Myler on the attack as the Kiwi defenders give chase. Note the low positioning of the BBC television cameras at the front of the grandstand.

any impact on the British nation. England had first entered it in 1950, only to suffer the indignity of being knocked out by losing to the U.S.A., and earlier in 1954 had gone out disappointingly in the quarter-finals in Switzerland. The first Rugby Union World Cup was still 33 years away, and cricket hadn't even thought of inventing a one-day game never mind playing a World Cup at it.

Yet here was our Rugby League team winning a World Cup for Britain for the very first time in any sport, they were doing it in one of the world's most famous and romantic capital cities, and they were seen doing it live on television back home in the U.K.

However, instead of rejoicing at the exploits of Valentine and his men, and recognising the huge opportunity Rugby League had opened up for itself after the first World Cup Final in Paris in 1954, all the folks back home in England could do was complain about how

Great Britain the winners in 1972 and captain Clive Sullivan is carried on the lap of honour in the Stade de Gerland, Lyon by Steve Nash and Mick Stephenson along with team-mates Bob Irving, Paul Charlton, Phil Lowe, George Nicholls, Brian Lockwood, John Holmes and Terry Clawson.

WORLD CUP FINALS
The venues
1954 - Parc des Princes, Paris
1968 - Sydney Cricket Ground
1970 - Headingley, Leeds
1972 - Stade de Gerland, Lyon
1977 - Sydney Cricket Ground
1988 - Eden Park, Auckland
1992 - Wembley Stadium, London
1995 - Wembley Stadium, London
2000 - Old Trafford, Manchester

much the television coverage had hit the crowds at their local clubs.

Since that memorable first tournament, the Rugby League World Cup has had a chequered history - good and bad - unable to establish itself with any regular pattern when it was crying out to be put on the calendar once every four years. Twelve tournaments have been staged to date, under varying formats, with Australia winning nine of them and Great Britain the other three. Only nine World Cup Finals have been contested, with the title being decided on three occasions on a first-past-the-post league table basis. Of those nine Finals, Australia has been in eight; Great Britain in six; and both France and New Zealand in two each without ever winning the World Cup. And, for the record, the three British captains who have lifted the Worl Cup have been: Dave Valentine, Eric Ashton and Clive Sullivan.

The Great Tours

(Above) A re-union in the late 1940s of all the British Lions touring team captains up to that time - they were, left to right: Jim Brough, James Lomas, Jonty Parkin, Jim Sullivan and Gus Risman. These men who had earned the highest accolade in the Rugby League game, comprised of two Welshman, two Cumbrians and a Yorkshireman. One other Lions captain missing on this occasion was the much admired Harold Wagstaff, who had passed away in 1939 at the far too young age of just 48.

THE pioneering visit by A.H.Baskerville and his "All Golds from New Zealand in 1907, followed a year later by the first Kangaroos from Australia, laid the foundations for international Rugby League as we came to know it. By 1910, the officials of the Northern Union were ready to accept the momentous challenge of sending their first touring team down-under to Australia and New Zealand.

As James "Jumbo" Lomas, a native of Maryport in Cumberland, and his British team set sail on the high seas bound for Australia in 1910, they embarked on an adventure that would establish something that became a wonderful part of Rugby League's tradition - and they also cemented the very future and ongoing prosperity of the Northern Union (later, the Rugby League.)

The four-yearly cycle of tours was interupted only by two World Wars and became the major attraction and incentive for every man good enough to play for a senior club as well as a vital and lucrative source of revenue for the British game's governing body.

Lions tours were great adventures as they took the British teams to many of the small towns in the Australian outback and as far as the South Island of New Zealand. The adventure was even greater in the days before air-travel became the norm and the tourists had to spend several weeks sailing to and from Australia via the Suez or Panama canals. The first Great Britain team to fly to Australia was the 1954 side captained by Dickie Williams, but it still took them the best part of a week to make the journey - however, they weren't the first Rugby League team to travel by aeroplane across the world, that achievement belonged to the first French touring team in 1951.

Much of Rugby League folklore was built on the achievements of our Lions touring teams as they battled to win the mythical "Ashes" on Australian soil. There has been no greater legend in the history of the game than the *"Rorke's Drift"* Test by Wagstaff and his men in 1914; and after that came such as the achievements of *"The Indomitables"* of 1946 who travelled by aircraft-carrier to Australia and the heroics of Alan Prescott and his team in the *"Battle for Brisbane"* in 1958. Once again, Rugby League led the way for British sport.

All the British Lions tour captains

1910 - James Lomas (Salford)	**1950 - Ernest Ward** (Bradford N'thn.)	**1984 - Brian Noble** (Bradford N'thn)
1914 - Harold Wagstaff (Huddersfield)	**1954 - Dickie Williams** (Hunslet)	**1988 - Ellery Hanley** (Wigan)
1920 - Harold Wagstaff (Huddersfield)	**1958 - Alan Prescott** (St.Helens)	**1990 - Mike Gregory** (Warrington)
1924 - Jonty Parkin (Wakefield Trin.)	**1962 - Eric Ashton** (Wigan)	*(To New Zealand & Papua.N.G. only)*
1928 - Jonty Parkin (Wakefield Trin.)	**1966 - Harry Poole** (Leeds)	**1992 - Ellery Hanley** (Wigan)
1932 - Jim Sullivan (Wigan)	**1970 - Frank Myler** (St.Helens)	**1996 - Andrew Farrell** (Wigan)
1936 - Jim Brough (Leeds)	**1974 - Chris Hesketh** (Salford)	*(To New Zealand, P.N.G. & Fiji only)*
1946 - Gus Risman (Salford)	**1979 - Doug Laughton** (Widnes)	

Great Britain v Papua New Guinea
1987 at Wigan - Andy Gregory on the attack.

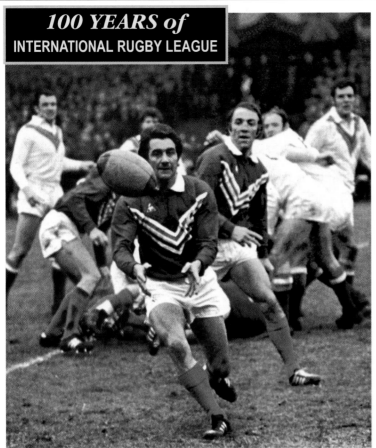

France v Great Britain
1971 at Toulouse - Roger Garrigues launches "les Bleus."

Great Britain v New Zealand
1985 at Wigan - Harry Pinner captains the British.

Australia v Great Britain
1992 at Brisbane - Mal Meninga and Shaun Edwards in a tense battle for the Ashes.

Australia v Great Britain
1984 at the Sydney Cricket Ground - Andy Goodway leads.

France v New Zealand
1989 at Carcassonne - David Fraisse - the French flair.

Britain's modern day stars

World Cup 1995 - England v Wales
The 1995 World Cup was a highspot for the international game. Pictured (above) England's Phil Clarke on the attack, supported by Bobbie Goulding and Denis Betts, in the semi-final against Wales at Old Trafford, Manchester.

The Super League era
British Rugby League's switch to a summer season in the years post 1995 has had a profound effect on the international game's ability to schedule Test series and tours. Despite the difficulties and disappointments for Great Britain, new stars came to the fore to establish their reputations at international level, notably Paul Sculthorpe (pictured left, playing versus New Zealand and Stuart Fielden (pictured above, playing in his Test debut against France.)

The French Flair

Pictured *(left)* PUIG-AUBERT, the most famous French player of them all, captured in his swashbuckling attacking style playing for France in an 8-3 win over the redoubtable Other Nationalities team in January 1950. On his left coming up in support is winger Vincent Cantoni. This match was typical of the time, played in front of a 30,000 crowd at the Velodrome stadium in Marseille, the great Mediterranean city which took Rugby League to its heart.

INTERNATIONAL Rugby League took on a whole new meaning in 1934 with the arrival of France on the scene. Immediately the European game had a new shape with an annual international tournament and many inter-club visits, as the French brought a colour and excitement to the game which was perfectly suited to their flair and desire to play open, attacking rugby.

In five years the game spread like wildfire in France, with the French team becoming European champions in 1939 after winning on English soil for the first time at St.Helens, inspired by their first superstar, Max Rousie.

Banned by Rugby Unionist in the Vichy government during World War two, Rugby League in France made a miraculous recovery after 1945 to enjoy its golden decade of success. The highlight of that was their first tour down-under, in which they hammered the Australians in Sydney and left an indelible impression on the Aussie crowds. The brightest star in that 1951 team full of stars led by manager Antoine Blain, was chunky little full-back Puig-Aubert of Carcassonne. They arrived home from the tour to a ticker-tape procession through the streets of Marseille - the great southern city which was such a stronghold for the Rugby League game then, along with Bordeaux and Lyon.

France staged the first World Cup in 1954 and repeated their Test series success in Australia on their second tour in 1955, captained by Jacques Merquey. Their famous tricolour jerseys became a symbol of razzle-dazzle football, with excitement and controversy in large doses.

(Above) In the huddle with the great French "world champions" team of 1951 as they take their half-time lemons during the match against New Zealand at the Parc des Prince in Paris. This was France's first international in their captial city after returning as heroes from Australia in 1951. Two vital figures in the history of the game stand, wearing overcoats, in the centre of the team - Paul Barriere (with hat) the President of the League and Antoine Blain, ex-international player and tour manager extraordinaire. Jean Dop is the player right next to them taking a drink. Puig-Aubert (number one) sits with his back to camera.

HIGH FLYING

TREVOR LAKE (Wigan)
versus Hunslet in 1965.

ALAN SKENE (Wakefield)
versus Warrington in 1962

St.Helens winger Tom Van Vollenhoven may have been the finest South African to grace the Rugby League game, but he was joined in England by many other exciting threequarters from the land of the Springboks in the late 1950s and early '60s - and all appeared to love the most spectacular approach to scoring a try, as the pictures on these pages show.

SPRINGBOKS

PIET PRETORIOUS (Workington)
versus Widnes in 1962

WILF ROSENBERG (Leeds)
versus St.Helens in 1961

Both Trevor Lake and Alan Skene got the chance to show their finishing skills on the game's biggest stage at Wembley, playing for Wigan and Wakefield Trinity respectively. Wilf Rosenberg was outstanding for Leeds in their first ever Championship winning season in 1960-61, whilst Piet Pretorious only stayed a couple of years with Workington Town after being taken to Derwent Park by Tom Mitchell, but he left indelible memories among the Cumbrian fans.

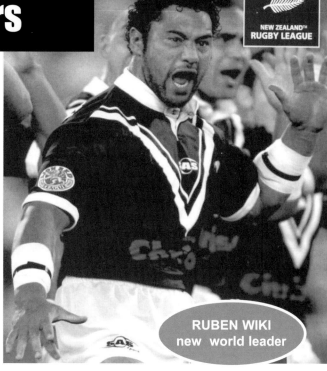

RUBEN WIKI
new world leader

NEW Zealander Ruben Wiki became the most capped player in the history of international Rugby League in 2005. After leading the Kiwis to victory in the Tri-Nations tournament and their match with France in the autumn of that year, Wiki proudly became the first man anywhere in the world to reach the half-century of caps for his country.

Only injury prevented Ruben taking his total up to 51 in the 2006 Anzac Test against Australia. He made his international debut for New Zealand back in 1994 against Papua New Guinea.

In reaching the 50-cap milestone, the powerful Kiwi warrior overtook French hero Gilbert Benausse who achieved 49 games for France in a wonderful international career which lasted from 1951 to 1964.

For the other two major Test playing nations, Great Britain and Australia, their lists of leading internationals are headed by Mick Sullivan and Garry Schofield, and Mal Meninga respectively. British stars Sullivan and Schofield share their ranking with 46 caps apiece, although the latter includes two substitute appearance in his total. Mick Sullivan also played in another three full internationals for Great Britain against France, but these came in the years before matches against the French were afforded full Test status by the British Rugby League. Mal Meninga heads the Australian list with 45 caps - a total which began in 1982 and ended at the conclusion of his record fourth Kangaroo tour in 1994.

Ruben Wiki's achievement in reaching 50 caps in the modern game, and overtaking such legends as Meninga, Benausse and Sullivan in the process, is one to be very proud of. Will anyone ever overtake it? Time will tell.

Australia
MAL MENINGA

France
GILBERT BENAUSSE

Great Britain
MICK SULLIVAN

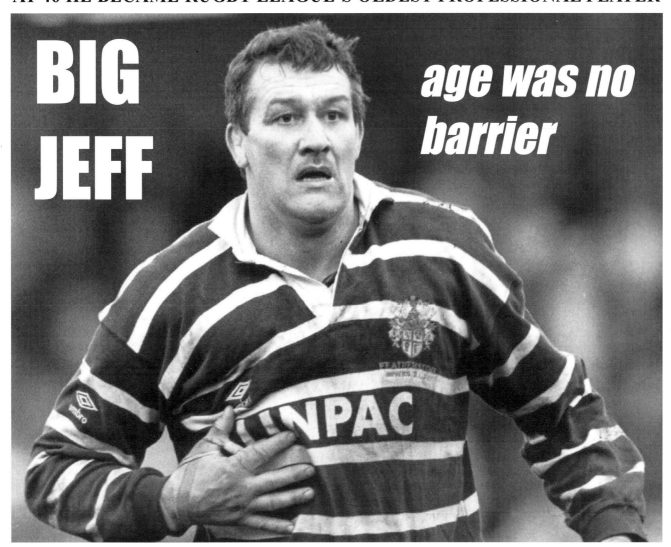

BIG JEFF

age was no barrier

THEY say that Rugby League is a young man's game and certainly in the modern era of full-time professionals at the top level, playing careers are likely to get even shorter. But for Jeff Grayshon, age certainly proved to be no barrier to him enjoying a wonderful career way past the normal "sell by" date expected in the professional game.

Big Jeff holds the record for being the oldest man to play first team professional Rugby League, as he last laced on his boots at the grand old age of 46, playing for Batley in 1995. He had begun his career in senior football 26 years earlier at Dewsbury, and in between played for Bradford, Leeds and Featherstone Rovers. Jeff was born on 4th March 1949.

In total he made 776 appearances in senior football, to stand fourth in the all-time records of the game behind the trio of "Hall of Fame" members: Jim Sullivan, Gus Risman and Neil Fox. Grayshon also holds the accolade of being the the oldest man to play Test Rugby League for Great Britain, which he did at the age of 36 years, eight months, against New Zealand at Elland Road, Leeds in November 1985. He was later selected to play against France in 1986, but was forced to withdraw due to injury.

Jeff won 13 Test caps in all after making his debut on the 1979 Lions tour. He had earlier played for England, including in the 1975 World Championship. Highlights of his club career included Dewsbury's famous Championship Final win in 1973 and further titles with Bradford Northern - but, alas, he never got to play at Wembley, leaving one major ambition unfulfilled.

By playing until he was 46 in 1995, Jeff Grayshon took over the mantle as the game's oldest player from the great Cumbrian forward of the early Northern Union days, Joe Ferguson, who was aged 44 when he played his last game for Oldham in 1923. Close behind Ferguson in longevity was the great Gus Risman, who was 43 when he finally called a halt to his marvellous career which included captaining Workington Town to victory at Wembley at the age of 41.

FOOTNOTE: It is not recorded in any of the game's official records, but we can claim to have seen the Welshman Frank Wilson play in a first team match for Runcorn, whilst he was their coach, in the autumun of 1985. Of no great interest if we accept the official records of the St.Helens club that Frank was born in April 1944 and thus was 24 years of age when he signed for them in 1968. But we also saw Frank claim to be 40 years-of-age when he played in Salford's centenary match in 1979. If that be true, Frank would also have been 46 in '85.

SAINTS

the name on that CUP

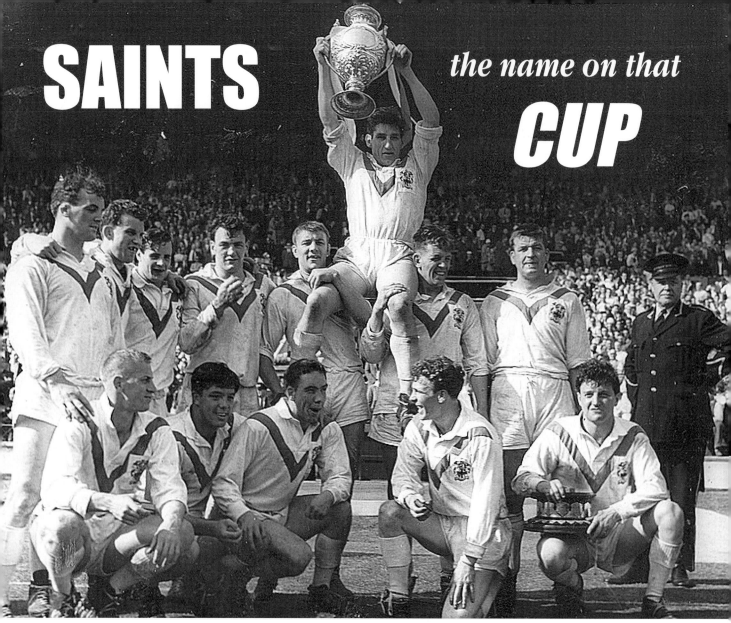

St.Helens, the Challenge Cup winners in 1961, in one of Wembley's most scorching occasions, with captain Vince Karalius helt aloft with the trophy. The victorious Saints players are, left to right, *(Standing):* Don Vines, Mick Sullivan, Alex Murphy, Cliff Watson, Dick Huddart, Karalius, Bob Dagnall, Abe Terry. *(In front):* Tom Van Vollenhoven, Brian McGinn, Wilf Smith, Ken Large and Austin Rhodes. Saints had just beaten local rivals Wigan, 12-6, to win the Cup for the second time in their history.

ST.HELENS love to put their name on the Challenge Cup and they did it again in 2006 - beating Huddersfield 42-12 in this year's final which was played at Twickenham after the much anticipated return to Wembley failed to materialise due to the new stadium not being ready.

In doing so, Saints confirmed their place as the game's dominant club in the Super League era, winning the Challenge Cup for the fifth time since 1996. And their livewire scrum-half Sean Long became the first man in the history of the game to win the Lance Todd Trophy for a third time. Long and his colleagues were following in some famous foosteps in the Saints teams which have put their name on the Cup in the past. This 2006 triumph was the tenth time in their history that St.Helens have won the Challenge Cup and it came exactly fifty years on from the first - that was in 1956 when Alan Prescott captained them to victory over Halifax.

THE 2006 CHALLENGE CUP FINAL
Played at Twickenham, Saturday 26th August 2006
ST.HELENS beat HUDDERSFIELD 42-12
(Half-time: 12-6)
St.Helens: Tries: Wilkin (2), Talau, Long, Fa'asavalu, Lyon, Cayless. **Goals:** Lyon (7).
Huddersfield: Tries: Aspinwall, Paul. **Goals:** De Vere (2)
ST.HELENS: Paul Wellens; Ade Gardner, Jamie Lyon, Willie Talau, Francis Meli; Leon Pryce, Sean Long; Paul Anderson, Keiron Cunningham, Jason Cayless, Jon Wilkin, Paul Sculthorpe (Capt.), Jason Hooper. *Subs.:* Lee Gilmour, James Roby, James Graham, Maurie Fa'asavalu.
HUDDERSFIELD: Paul Reilly; Martin Aspinwall, Chris Nero, Michael De Vere, Stuart Donlan; Chris Thorman (Capt.), Robbie Paul; Paul Jackson, Brad Drew, Jim Gannon, Eorl Crabtree, Andy Raleigh, Stephen Wild. *Subs.:* Steve Snitch, Stuart Jones, Paul Smith, Wayne McDonald.
Referee: Mr. Richard Silverwood (Dewsbury)
Attendance: 65,187.

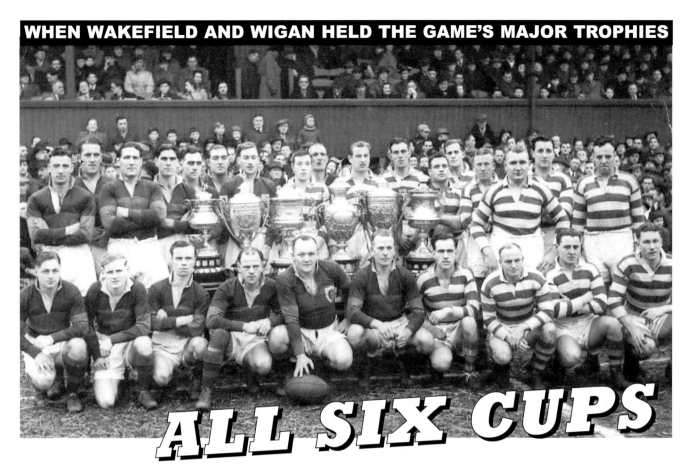

ALL SIX CUPS

THE photograph (above) is a famous one in the annals of Rugby League history. Taken on 4th January, 1947, at Belle Vue, Wakefield, it pictures the two teams who at that time were holders of all six of the game's major trophies. And the players of Wakefield Trinity and Wigan were proud to display those trophies before playing each other that day - Trinity holders of the Challenge Cup, Wigan the Championship, and each club holders of their respective County Cup and League.

The players, with Wakefield in the dark jerseys and Wigan (of course) in the cherry and white hoops, line up as follows on the picture:

Left to right: *(Standing):* **Baddeley, Higgins, Exley, Longley, Marson, Booth, Howes, Blan J., Bratley, Atkinson, Blan W., Shovaton, Ratcliffe, Lawrenson, Banks G., Ward, Woosey.** *(In front):* **Brooks, Banks W., Perry, Stott, Wilkinson, Teall, Cunliffe, Mountford, Toohey & Nordgren.**

The presence of the six major trophies, from which the famous "All Four Cups" were available to any single club in a season but which were won, as history tells us, by only three - Hunslet, Huddersfield and Swinton - is a reminder of the rare group of players who managed to win all six medals. Only a handful managed it by playing with successful clubs on both sides of the Pennines and thus being in teams victorious in both Lancashire and Yorkshire Cups and Leagues. This distinguished group who won all six medals included:

AUBREY CASEWELL - the giant Welsh forward who played for both Salford and Leeds in the years before World War Two. After the war, Aubrey became Secretary of the Leeds and District Amateur Rugby League.

ALAN EDWARDS - the Welsh winger who was one of Lance Todd's Red Devils of Salford in pre-war years and then completed his medal collection with Bradford Northern (post-war.)

TED SLEVIN - the solid prop-forward who played for Wigan and then transferred to Huddersfield, giving many years of fine service to Fartown and completing his set of all six medals with the Championship in 1962.

DEREK TURNER - the loose-forward who combined toughness with subtle handling and kicking skills, "Rocky" starred for Oldham before returning to his native Yorkshire to captain the successful Wakefield Trinity team of the early 'sixties.

JOHN ETTY - the powerful winger who followed the same path as Turner, winning Lancashire Cup and League medals, plus the Championship, with Oldham before joining Wakefield and winning at Wembley in 1960 and also picking up the Yorkshire Cup and League titles with Trinity.

Can any of our readers remember any other players who won all six medals? The opportunity to win them, along with the coveted "All Four Cups" ended after the 1972-73 season when the Rugby League split into two divisions and thus abandoned the old County Leagues within the Northern Rugby League Championship. In the years that followed, more major trophies and medal winning opportunities were introduced, like the Premiership and the John Player (later Regal) Trophy. But in the folklore of Rugby League, the legend of "All Four Cups" always retained its place and remained undiminished.

YOU'VE GOT TO LAUGH!

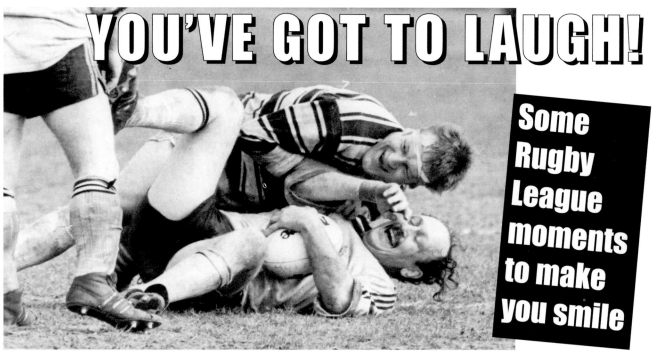

Some Rugby League moments to make you smile

(Above) Yorkshire rivals Charlie Stone and Brian Lockwood share a joke as they crashed to the ground together in a match between Hull and Widnes. Maybe it was a Cas'-Featherstone joke?

LONG tours overseas were the breeding ground of so many of Rugby League's funniest moments and dramatic tales. But touring could be tough on the players. Billy Smith, the great little Aussie half-back on the 1967 Kangaroo tour, was never far away from trouble, and he nearly went too far one morning at their tour base of Ilkley. Billy tells the story:

"Kevin Junee went away on the tour as the other half-back with me, but he went away with a busted ankle so he couldn't play. So I played the first 12 or 14 games straight. They played Monday, Wednesday, Friday. You play every club side you can get. You're travelling and you're training and I was getting belted and getting tired - and I was getting cranky. They made me get up one morning for training at 6 o'clock. I had a cut ear, a cut eye, a corked leg. They said, *'You've got to go training.'* I said, *'I can't. I can hardly walk.'* But they made me run up over the moor and they were all having breakfast when I got back so I threw a big house brick through the window and straight into Reg Gasnier's cornflakes, of all things. They were going to send me home after that!"

AND coping with referees from the home country was always another source of incident and amusing stories for touring teams. Noel Kelly, who made three Kangaroo tours to Europe, and was a real "hard head" of the Australian pack - as well as one of its funniest characters - recalled the 1967 Test against Great Britain at Swinton in the snow.

"Referee Fred Lindop sent me off, alleging a stiff-arm tackle - even though it missed by a mile. Tommy Bishop was the player involved and little Tom took the best dive you've ever seen. I didn't get within feet of him but Tommy jumped up in the air and rolled over -

and Lindop sent me off. Lindop later cliamed that my tackle '***would*** have taken Bishop's head off.'"

EARLIER in the same game Noel Kelly provided an insight into how things use to "work" in the scrums in those days, when he claimed Tommy Bishop was putting the ball in his own feet all the time, and not putting the ball anywhere *near* the scrum on his feed. "So," recalled Kelly, "I said to Denis Manteit, one of my props: 'Next scrum, I'm going to belt the hooker.' I did just that, hanging one on my opposite number, Peter 'Flash' Flanagan. Flash had a whinge, and I said to him: 'You'll get more if you don't tell that little asshole to put the ball in the scrum.' Next scrum, Tommy put it under the loose-forward's feet, so I belted Flash again. 'Is this what I'm going to get every time I win the scrum?' said Flash. 'Just tell him,' I said. Anyhow, it worked, things got better and we started winning the ball - and the Test match."

WHEN the famous Great Britain loose-forward Malcolm Reilly went to play in Australia for the Manly club, he was often a target for the sensation-seeking Sydney media. To the point that when Mal's troublesome knee injury threatened to keep him out of a big match, one local radion station even set up a spoof interview with "Malcolm Reilly's knee." And guess what? The knee spoke with a Yorkshire accent.

TERRY CLAWSON, tough forward, top goal-kicker, World Cup winner and successful author, was well known for his dry sense of humour. In one match playing for Featherstone Rovers against Hull at the Boulevard, Terry found himself intercepting a Hull pass inside his own "25." Now Terry was a big lad and the thought of running the length of the field to score a try wasn't part of his natural game. But, bravely he set off downfield, expecting to be tackled after making a few valuable yards. However, for some strange reason, he discovered a previously unknown burst of speed and kept holding off all retreating defenders as he kept looking over his shoulder waiting to be brought down. Eventually, as Terry crossed the Hull "25" a winger flew in from the touchline and caught up with Clawson, finally bringing him to ground just ten yards short of the line. As the Hull crowd gave a massive sigh of relief, Terry turned to the bloke who'd just tackled and said: *"What kept you?"*

(Above) Frank Collier playing for Widnes brings down Hull K.R.'s Eric Palmer at Wembley in 1964. Frank would often have his fellow players in stiches.

PLAYERS could incur the wrath of referees for many reasons - Alex Murphy just had to look at "Sergeant Major" Eric Clay - but this one takes the (dog) biscuit. Playing in a youth match once, a Yorkshire lad who became a very well known forward especially with the Hunslet and Bramley clubs, got sent off by the ref. for feeding a dog on the touchline.

ANOTHER incident with an animal - although this one not funny - involved the great old Cumbrian forward Douglas Clark, of Fartown and *"Rorke's Drift"* fame.

A champion wrestler as well as a champion rugby footballer, tales of Duggy's great strength were legend in his native Cumberland. And one story concerned him breaking the neck of a stubborn bull in a field in Patterdale in the Lake District. Douglas was out walking with his dog, apparently unaware of the bull's presence until he was about to open a gate and leave the field, when the dog barked to warn him of the impending danger. As Clark turned he found himself face to face with the powerful animal and his back just a few feet from the gate.

As the bull move towards him, Douglas instinctively gripped its horns intending to twist its head and wrestle it to the ground, and then make his escape from the field before the bull regained its feet. But, unfortunately, this did not happen as the bull would not give in to the "throw," and held its ground. This meant Clark had to use his powerful arms to try and bring the animal down which resulted in its neck being broken.

This tale became legend in Patterdale but, apparently, Douglas Clark himself - although he would never deny the incident taking place - was such an animal lover that he was very upset at the bull's fate and would avoid talking about it.

ENGLISH clubs have always loved signing Aussie players but some got more than they bargained for when they tried to recruit well known prankster Paul "Fatty" Vautin.

"Fatty" tells the story of when his Manly team came over to play Wigan in that famous match in 1987 and the trip became a "smorgasbord" for the English club directors trying to sign up players. Vautin was sitting on his bed in the hotel one afternoon when there was a knock at the door. When he opened it he was confronted by a man aged about 40 and the other a bit older. "The old bloke had the thickest glasses I've ever seen in my life," said Vautin. "They came in and the young bloke sat the other one down in a chair and I sat on the bed. The old bloke did the talking."

"Paul," he said. "I'm chairman of the Leigh football club and we'd loove you to join us, lad. How does 10,000 pounds sound?" Vautin raised his hand and waved. "Excuse me," he said, "I'm over here. He was talking to the cupboard the whole time."

Soon after "Fatty" thanked the men for their offer and saw them to the door, a few minutes later there was another knock. "This time it was Widnes coach Doug Laughton," Vautin said. "He walked in with Dale Shearer who he'd also just approached to sign for Widnes, and wanted me too. I virtually agreed to terms but in the end they 'brushed' me and I never heard any more about it. But that was what was going on all over the hotel, the Pommie coaches and secretaries were wandering up and down the corridors trying to sign anyone they could get their hands on. They thought it was Christmas."

FRANK Collier of Wigan (and later Widnes) was one of the funniest blokes to play Rugby League. One humourous tale about Frank concerned playing at Wembley in the Challenge Cup Final and the strict protocol required when shaking hands with Prince Philip in the pre-match presentation.

All the players were told of their impending meeting with Royalty that "Under no circumstances must you speak to the Prince unless he speaks to you first ." But when the Queen's husband duly came to Frank in the line-up, the Wigan lad stuck out his big coal-miner's hand to greet Prince Philip, shook hands warmly and said with a big smile: "Alright sir, how's the wife and kids?" At which point, Frank claimed, the shocked Prince replied: "Fine thanks, how about your's?"

STARS KNEW THEIR WORTH

THROUGHOUT the history of Rugby League the game has thrived on quick-witted players and, almost inevitably, those who were the smartest, most opportunist, footballers on the field of play were also the sharpest wheeler-dealers off it.

For a sport that owed its very birth to the need to pay "broken time" money to working-class footballers, it was no surprise that some of the most talented players from that background should realise their potential as crowd-pulling "stars" and seek to gain greater financial rewards in return for their ability to generate lucrative gate-money.

And as soon as the clubs established their long-held search for personalities by signing men from Rugby Union or from Australasia, the die was cast for a constant battle for "home grown" players to be paid anything like their true worth compared to the lucrative terms offered to those "imports." The stark contrast between "locals" and "imports" was always made more acute by the registration system laid down by the Rugby Football League in the nine decades before a so-called "freedom of contract" was introduced, which stated that all secondary payments to players were illegal.

The great BILLY BATTEN pictured with the Yorkshire Cup in 1924.

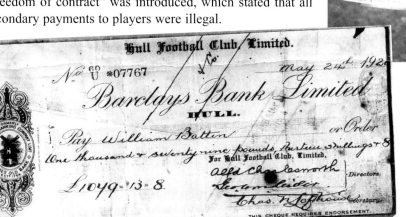

(Pictured left) The original cheque for £1,079, 13 shillings and 8 pence, presented to Billy Batten, as the result of his Benefit Match, Hull versus York, on 3rd April, 1920.

This meant that once a player had signed for a senior club and was deemed a "professional," he could expect no further lump-sum "contract" payments for the rest of his career. The only legally approved incentive was for a man to give ten year's unbroken service to a club and then he could expect a benefit - and the only alternative to biding your time was to become a bit of a rebel.

Of the nine original inductees to the Rugby League Hall of Fame, three were Welshmen and two Australians. Of the remaining four who came from Yorkshire and Lancashire, three players from different eras (Billy Batten, Jonty Parkin and Alex Murphy) all found themselves involved in controversies as they sought to better themselves. In short, they all knew their own worth - in sharp contrast to the fourth member of that legendary quartet, the great Harold Wagstaff, about whom one has never been able to read any suggestion that arguments over

(Right) JONTY PARKIN, the international team captain who was so sure of his own value that he paid his own transfer-fee to change clubs.

moneytary reward should come between him and giving loyal service to the claret and gold of Huddersfield.

Billy Batten was the sport's first real "superstar" long before that term was invented - he was also its most controversial character in the era before and after the First World War. After establishing his reputation in Hunslet's "All Four Cups" team of 1907-08 and also on the very first Lions tour to Australasia in 1910, Billy soon recognised that he was worth a lot more money than he had hitherto been paid for playing Northern Union football.

He had received a new suit, apparently valued at £5, but no money to sign as a professional for Hunslet. At the height of his fame with the Parksiders he was on excellent terms for the time of £2-10 shillings for a win and £2 for a loss. But Billy claimed to have been offered £4 a week all year round by Manchester United to be a soccer player, and he had got wind of some of the figures other Northern Union teams were paying to their imports from Australia and New Zealand.

Quite understandably, Billy Batten was aggrieved, believing he had not been getting what he was worth at Hunslet. He refused to play for them and his stayaway dispute became a source of controversy and intrigue throughout the north. A transfer to Hull would make him the highest paid player in the Northern Union by some distance - this, coupled with a £600 transfer fee which was double the previous world record fee of £300 paid by Oldham to Salford for the 1910 Lions tour captain Jim Lomas, was a risky gamble on the part of the "Airlie Birds," but it paid off handsomely.

ALEX MURPHY - got a signing-on fee of just £80 from St.Helens when other leading schoolboy players of the time were commanding fees of £1,000. Alex, like Batten and Parkin, had to fight to get his true worth.

Batten was paid £14 a match by Hull - a phenomenal amount for the time - but the club was happy because Billy's presence in their team put thousands on the gate every week and easily paid off their investment in him. Meanwhile, his much lesser paid team-mates appeared to be happy for the great man to get such rewards as that old chestnut about him "putting winning money in our pockets" rang true around the Boulevard.

There was much disbelief that Batten was actually paid £14 a match, but in later years Hull officials of that time confirmed that he was. A few years earlier, Billy had earned just one shilling a day down the pit, and there were many reports of his great generosity with his new found wealth - during the depression years he was known to buy food and give money to the villagers in his native Kinsey and Fitzwilliam, including giving a significant proportion of the benefit he had received from Hull in 1920.

Batten was presented with a benefit cheque for over £1,079 - a huge amount of money for the time. Compare that with the £2,000 or so which Alex Murphy received from St.Helens over 46 years later and you realise the full extent of Billy Batten's popularity ... and his worth.

Another "Hall of Famer" from the same neck of the woods as Billy Batten, was Jonty Parkin - and he was another man who knew his worth and proved to be as smart an operator off the field as he was on it. Jonty was a pit worker at the age of 16 and a professional player, but he developed into a very successful businessman after establishing his reputation as one of the game's greatest scrum-halves and captains.

Just like Billy Batten, Parkin decided to take charge of his own destiny after 17 years with Wakefield Trinity when, in 1930, the club committee decided that all their players would be paid a flat rate. For many years Jonty had been paid more than all the others and he did not want to accept the new terms. So Trinity put him on the transfer list for £100 and within 24 hours, Jonty himself had paid them that amount and bought his own transfer - effectively making him a free agent in the days when players were tied "for life" to the club that held their registration. He wasted little time in agreeing much more lucrative terms of £10 a match with Hull Kingston Rovers and set about using his two seasons on Humberside to start a fish-selling business which he developed very successfully.

After seeing Jonty Parkin "buy" his own transfer to Hull K.R., the Rugby League Council immediately changed their laws to stop such a thing happening again.

Over three decades later Alex Murphy, the man often described as the modern day Jonty Parkin, found himself walking down a similar path when he decided the time had come to leave Knowsley Road and his home-town club St.Helens. It was 1966, and Alex had just turned down the chance to go on his third Lions tour to Australia - citing business reasons, but many believed the fact that he was not made captain of the touring team also played a part. He had led Saints to a Cup and League "double" in '66 but was unhappy at being forced to play out of position at centre. Murphy shocked St.Helens by announcing he was going to emigrate to Australia, but the Saints directors' shock soon turned to smiles when they learned that the North Sydney club were prepared to pay a transfer fee approaching their world record £12,000 valuation of Alex.

Imagine their disappointment when, at the eleventh hour, Alex had a change of heart and announced that he had settled for a £30-a-week, five year agreement with Leigh to be their team-manager. And, as long as Leigh didn't register him as a player, St.Helens wouldn't get a penny in transfer-fees, nor could they prevent him taking up his new job. It wasn't quite like Jonty Parkin buying his own transfer, but it certainly forced Saints' hand - and, eventually, Leigh and St.Helens did reach an agreement on a fee to allow Murphy to become a player at Hilton Park, so everybody was happy.

Not that St.Helens could ever have complained about getting value for money out of Alex Murphy - as they had paid him just £80 to sign for them as a 16-year-old and he became the man voted "player of the 20th Century."

(Above) Look at the sheer joy on the faces of the spectators who knew they had just seen something very special. St.Helens star Tom Van Vollenhoven is mobbed by delighted fans after scoring his brilliant try in the 1959 Championship Final against Hunslet. It was rated one of the finest tries ever seen in a big game, in which the South African flyer had left a trail of Hunslet defenders in his wake on an 80-yard miracle movement along the Odsal touchline.

Hunslet and Saints served up a scorcher

THE modern day Super League Grand Finals are continuing a wonderful tradition in Rugby League of end-of-season play-offs and a major final to decide the Championship title. Of course there is something *slightly* different about the present day system of having a top six play-off from a division with only 12 teams, compared to the old top-four play-off which used to be so revered in Rugby League. Then, the top-four came from one big division containing all the professional clubs, up to 30 of them. It was every club's "Holy Grail" to make the top-four and, as a system of deciding the Champions

rather than the first-past-the-post system employed in soccer, it had much merit because every club did not get to play each other and there were two "regional conferences" within the Northern Rugby League in the shape of the Lancashire and Yorkshire County Leagues.

The Championship play-offs began to lose much of their crowd-pulling appeal after they were watered down to a top-16 play-off commencing in 1965. That followed two seasons of the League being split into two divisions, a system that was abandoned just two years into its proposed three-year trial as it had quickly become apparent the damage it was doing to the game as a whole. Much of that damage coming from the loss of the Championship Final itself which had previously been such a prestigious event and big money-spinner. It was no coincidence that, when the game was again split into divisions - seemingly forever - commencing in 1973-74, with the Champions being the team finishing top of the First Division, the Rugby League immediately introduced a Premiership tournament to preserve its concept of end of season play-offs climaxing in a second major Final.

For many years, the Championship Final complimented the earlier Challenge Cup Final at Wembley and brought the curtain down as the *grand finale* of the season. It also became tradition for supporters to believe the Championship Final produced a better game, between two guaranteed top sides and, perhaps, without the nerves of trying to put on a show at Wembley.

Just as staging the present-day Grand Finals at Old Trafford is a huge part of its spectator appeal, it was the decision to play the Championship Final on major soccer grounds which saw its attendances first rocket. That was back in the pre-War years and the Rugby League clubs themselves just did not have a stadium big enough to accomodate the crowds which wanted to watch the Final. Hence, in 1938 the Hunslet versus Leeds Championship Final was played within the city at the Elland Road stadium, home of Leeds United, drawing a crowd of 54,112 - a new record high for the game in this country. That was

THE NORTHERN RUGBY FOOTBALL LEAGUE

League Championship Final
——1959——

HUNSLET v. ST. HELENS

SATURDAY
16th MAY
1959
Kick-off 3.0 p.m.

At ODSAL STADIUM
BRADFORD

OFFICIAL SOUVENIR PROGRAMME - Price 6d.

followed a year later by playing at Manchester City's Maine Road ground, where Salford versus Castleford set another record attendance of 69,504 - a figure way higher than any which had attended the Challenge Cup Final - the huge Wembley crowds only began in the post-War "boom" years. Maine Road become the "traditional" home of Championship Finals until the development of Odsal Stadium gave the game a home of its "own" big enough to accomodate the crowds.

From 1957 to 1962 every Championship Final was played in May at Odsal and, of all the memorable games they provided, none could match the high-scoring epic between St.Helens and Hunslet in 1959. This was the match in which Saints' brilliant South African wingers Van Vollenhoven and Prinsloo, ran riot - Van Vollenhoven scoring a hat-trick which included the still talked about "wonder" try which saw him beat half the Hunslet team in an 80-yard run. For gallant Hunslet, who had surprisingly beaten Wigan at Central Park in the top-four play-off to get to the Final, it was a sign of their quality that they contributed so much to such a great attacking game against a St.Helens team full of international stars in thir pomp.

(Above) The 1957 Championship Final at Odsal Stadium and one unfortunate Hull defender feels the "force" of Oldham's rugged loose-forward Derek "Rocky" Turner, whilst on the left another great loose-forward, Johnny Whiteley, stands guard. Oldham won 15-14 to clinch the title for the last time. Attendance: 62,199.

GRAHAM LOWE remembers

Wigan's winning attitude

Coach Graham Lowe standing on the extreme left with his victorious Wigan team at Wembley in 1988 - they had just beaten Halifax to win the Challenge Cup. They are, left to right, *(Standing):* Lowe, Geoff Hurst (assistant coach), Ian Potter, Andy Goodway, Ellery Hanley, Shaun Wane, Kevin Iro, Joe Lydon, Henderson Gill, Ian Gildart, Adrian Shelford, Ian Lucas. *(In front):* Brian Case, Tony Iro, Nicky Kiss, Shaun Edwards, Steve Hampson, Ged Byrne, Andy Gregory and Dean Bell.

DURING 2006, in his role as a prominent sports-columnist in his native New Zealand, former Wigan coach Graham Lowe found himself discussing the rotation policy being operated by the All Blacks Rugby Union squad - and immediately cast his mind back to those heady days at Central Park.

"I'd be surprised if all the (All Black) players were happy with it," said Lowe. "I remember suggesting to the Wigan squad I coached that I was considering rotating a group of about 20 players.

"It nearly caused a strike because at that time players were paid for each winning game they played. No play, no pay.

"I clearly remember being aggressively questioned about the policy by Great Britain international Andy Goodway, one of our back-rowers. Shyness wasn't part of his nature, and he was as close to a union delegate as you could get. He said if he wasn't good enough to make the team on a regular basis, he wanted a transfer to another club who would appreciate his talent.

"I thought he was right and his argument was sound. After considering it for about 30 seconds, I decided to stick with the timeless method of picking the best each week. While I never got the chance to try the rotation system, the threat of it took the Wigan team to plenty of trophies. The other obvious factor was if we didn't put the best team on the park each week we were leaving ourselves open to get smashed by our rivals.

"At international level, I found that some players were happy just to get a jersey. Others, because of their competitive nature, preferred (and expected) to be in every Test side. It's the nature of the beast. Being second or third in line for any position can bring out the best in a player, but it can also cause a hidden resentment."

Graham Lowe certainly found the key to success with the great Wigan players in the late '80s.

Andy Goodway (left) with Graham Lowe and Wigan as Wembley winners in 1989 - Goodway was nicknamed "B.A." for "Bad Attitude," but he got the job done.

Flyer
OFFIAH

Martin Offiah, one of Great Britain's most successful wingers with 26 tries in 33 international appearances. He followed in the footsteps of all Britain's finest wingers of the past to blaze a trail in the modern game.

The **RUGBY LEAGUE** NEWS

HECTOR RAWSON
Co-Manager
British Team

TOM HESKETH
Co-Manager
British Team

FIRST TEST
AUSTRALIA
v
GREAT BRITAIN

Under the auspices of the
AUSTRALIAN RUGBY LEAGUE
BOARD OF CONTROL.

SYDNEY CRICKET GROUND.

JUNE 12th 1954.

Vol. 35. No. 15.

1/-

Registered in Australia for Transmission by post as a newspaper.

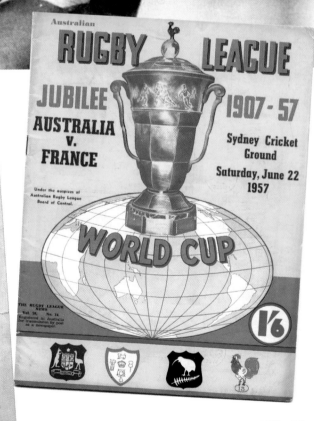

Australian
RUGBY LEAGUE
JUBILEE
AUSTRALIA V. FRANCE
1907 - 57

Sydney Cricket Ground
Saturday, June 22 1957

Under the auspices of
Australian Rugby League
Board of Control.

WORLD CUP

THE RUGBY LEAGUE NEWS
Vol. 38   No. 14.
Registered in Australia for transmission by post as a newspaper

1/6

Memories of Ashes Test matches and World Cups with these programmes from the 1950s.

WALES
keeps a
welcome

**JONATHAN
DAVIES**

DAVID WATKINS

(Pictured, right) The Wales team which played Australia at Ninian Park, Cardiff in October, 1982. The Aussies won 37-7 Left to right, *(Back row):* Paul Ringer, Martin Herdman, Tommy David, Glyn Shaw, Paul Prendiville, Brian Juliff. *(In front):* Steve Fenwick (Captain), Brynmor Williams, Chris Camilleri, John Bevan, Lyn Hopkins, Don Parry and Lyn Hallett.

New Crusaders launched in 2006

WALES had a professional Rugby League club again in 2006 with the launch of the Celtic Crusaders, who came into the game with high hopes they could build the kind of firm foundations for a League club in the Principality which have always proved so elusive in the past.

Based at the Brewery Field in Bridgend, the Crusaders have made it plain they hope to be able to bid for a Super League franchise in the future, but for the moment their hopes of rising up the divisions of the National League immediately didn't quite happen. Almost, but not quite, as the Crusaders went agonisingly close to reaching the National League Two Grand Final in their first season - by far the best performance of any of the League's new "expansionist" clubs to date.

The Welsh side were beaten by a "golden point" drop goal at home to Swinton in the semi-final, after the two teams had finished level after 20 minutes extra-time. That may have been a heart-breaker for the Crusaders' players, but it shouldn't take the shine off what had been a very good debut season in the professional ranks.

With Queenslander John Dixon their coach, the Crusaders had a strong backbone of talented Australian players running through their team - most notably two former stars of the Queensland Cup, full-back Tony Duggan and half-back Jace Van Dijk. The Aussies may have provided the experience all new clubs need, but the ultimate aim has to be all about developing Welsh Rugby League players and no less than 21 Welshmen tasted the game at professional level for the first time in 2006. That augers well for the future and is the positive result of having an established conference of amateur teams now playing the game in Wales.

That was something Rugby League did not have back in 1981 when the most high-profile of all its post-War Welsh clubs was launched, the Cardiff Blue Dragons. Then, the new club was able to gain big publicity by signing several Welsh Rugby Union internationals - among them Steve Fenwick, Tom David and Paul Ringer - and the experienced backbone came from the north of England, not Australia as it did in 2006. The other major difference between then and now was in crowd support - whilst the Celtic Crusaders numbered their crowds in just hundreds from the start, back in 1981 the Blue Dragons

WALES THEN AND NOW ...

(Above) The Welsh team take a half-time break whilst playing France in the Toulouse Stadium in 1963. Players in the picture include: Ray Glastonbury on the right, next to masseur Paddy Armour; the reserve Malcolm Davies wearing a coat and carrying a duffle-bag; and numbered players with their backs to the camera are Kel Coslett, Colin Dixon and Idwal Fisher. France won 23-3. *(Above, left)* An example of the very smart and up-beat approach to promoting themselves by the Celtic Crusaders club in their debut season in 2006.

were able to draw around 10,000 to their opening match at Ninian Park.

Establishing a presence for the game in Wales has long been an ambition for Rugby League, but - prior to the upheavals of 1995 - trying to set up teams in the Principality always had to face the hostile attitude and influence of Rugby Union. Happily, in 2006, that is not the case as the Rugby Union recognises that League is no threat to them.

It might be hard for modern days followers of the game to fully appreciate the absolutely huge influence Welsh players used to have in Rugby League. Whilst the records show that over 150 Welsh Rugby Union internationals made the switch to Rugby League, the total number of Welsh players to "go north" would stretch into thousands, such was the steady stream of men looking to the Rugby League (and formerly Northern Union) clubs to help provide them with a source of income.

Among the capped Welsh internationals who turned to Rugby League were some of the biggest stars in the Rugby Union game at that time, the so-called "golden boys" of Wales - including names like: Lewis Jones, Keith Jarrett, Terry Price, David Watkins, John Bevan, Terry Holmes and Jonathan Davies. Many more were not so well known in their own country but became hugely successful Rugby League players - among them three original members of the game's prestigious "Hall of Fame" - Gus Risman, Jim Sullivan and Billy Boston.

The
COUNTY CHAMPIONSHIP

TITLE WINNERS
LANCASHIRE 32
(plus 2 shared)
YORKSHIRE 22
(plus 2 shared)
CUMBERLAND 14
(plus 2 shared)
CHESHIRE 1

(Above) Cumberland versus Lancashire at Workington's Derwent Park in September 1967. Tommy Bishop is the man in possession for the Red Rose county as winger Bill Burgess awaits his pass. Cumberland's loose-forward Bill Pattinson moves in to tackle with winger Keith Davies standing guard. Lancashire won this game 19-6 on their way to the Championship.

FOR the first eight decades of Rugby League's life, the County Championship was a major part of the game's representative fixture list. Whilst inter-county matches may not have drawn the big crowds which were attracted to the top inter-club fixtures in Lancashire and Yorkshire, they were always a major incentive for the players. For some, they were a stepping stone towards international honours, for others winning a county cap would be the proudest moment of their footballing career.

Lancashire won the inaugural County Championship in the first season of the Northern Union in 1895-96. Some eighty-seven years later, the tournament was abandoned by the Rugby League after several seasons of diminishing interest in which the county games struggled to find a convenient place in the fixture list and to draw any kind of significant public support. Such a half-hearted approach was a sad end to a competition that had figured so strongly in the game's history.

In its latter years, the County Championship was most keenly supported by the Cumbrians, who did not have the big club events to support like their Yorkshire and Lancashire brethren. This was following a tradition established long before the county of Cumberland had any senior clubs in the professional ranks of the Northern Rugby League - including a famous hat-trick of Championship title wins in the 1930s. It was, perhaps, fitting that it was that great champion of the Cumbrian game, Tom Mitchell, who presented a trophy to be awarded to the winners of the County Championship beginning in 1966-67. In the years before that there was no trophy for the winners, just the prestige of being the champion county and those prized winners' medals for their players. Tom, along with other dedicated officials like "George" Hirst of Yorkshire and Frank Devonald of Lancashire, was a man who recognised the true appeal and value of a meaningful County Championship.

ALL THE RUGBY LEAGUE COUNTY CHAMPIONSHIP WINNERS

1895-96 Lancashire **1896-97** Lancashire **1897-98** Yorkshire **1898-99** Yorkshire **1899-1900** Lancashire
1900-01 Lancashire **1901-02** Cheshire **1902-03** Lancashire **1903-04** Lancashire **1904-05** Yorkshire
1905-06 Lancashire & Cumberland joint winners **1906-07** Lancashire **1907-08** Cumberland **1908-09** Lancashire
1909-10 Cumberland & Yorkshire joint winners **1910-11** Lancashire **1911-12** Cumberland **1912-13** Yorkshire
1913-14 Undecided **1919-20** Undecided **1920-21** Yorkshire **1921-22** Yorkshire
1922-23 Lancashire & Yorkshire joint winners **1923-24** Lancashire **1924-25** Lancashire **1925-26** Lancashire
1926-27 Lancashire **1927-28** Cumberland **1928-29** Lancashire **1929-30** Lancashire
1930-31 Yorkshire **1931-32** Lancashire **1932-33** Cumberland **1933-34** Cumberland

CUMBERLAND

Before a famous against-the-odds victory over Yorkshire at Whitehaven in September 1956. Left to right, *(Standing):* Jim Drake (Hull), Bill Smith (Whitehaven), Dick Huddart (Whitehaven), Jack Richardson (Workington), Geoff Robinson (Whitehaven), Steve McCourt (Whitehaven), Bill McAlone (Whitehaven). *(In front):* John McKeown (Whitehaven), Billy Garratt (Whitehaven), Jimmy Lewthwaite (Barrow) Captain, Sol Roper (Workington), Syd Lowden (Whitehaven) and Bill Drake (Hull).

LANCASHIRE

The County Championship was not held in 1977-78, but that didn't stop Lancashire playing Yorkshire in a Jubilee Roses match, which Lancashire won 33-8 at Naughton Park, Widnes. The Red Rose team that night in October 1977, was:
Left to right, *(Standing):* Mick Adams (Widnes), George Nicholls (St.Helens), John Woods (Leigh), Stuart Wright (Widnes), Alf Wilkinson (Leigh), Tony Gourley (Rochdale), Eric Prescott (Salford). *(In front):* Geoff Pimblett (St.Helens), Ken Gill (Salford), Keith Elwell (Widnes), Reg Bowden (Widnes) Captain, Mal Aspey (Widnes), Les Jones (St.Helens)

YORKSHIRE

Pictured (right) is the Yorkshire team which clinched the County Championship of 1946 by beating Lancashire 13-10 at Hunslet. The team from 1 to 13 was: Ledgard (Dewsbury); Williamson (Hunslet), Kitching (Bradford), Ward (Bradford), Longley (Featherstone); Rylance (Wakefield), Burnell (Keighley), G.Gronow (Halifax), Ramsden (Hull KR), Wilkinson (Wakefield), White (York), Booth (Hull) and Dockar (Hull KR).

1934-35 Cumberland **1935-36** Lancashire **1936-37** Lancashire **1937-38** Lancashire **1938-39** Lancashire
1945-46 Lancashire **1947-48** Yorkshire **1948-49** Cumberland **1949-50** Undecided **1950-51** Undecided
1951-52 Yorkshire **1952-53** Lancashire **1953-54** Yorkshire **1954-55** Yorkshire **1955-56** Lancashire
1956-57 Lancashire **1957-58** Yorkshire **1958-59** Yorkshire **1959-60** Cumberland **1960-61** Lancashire
1961-62 Cumberland **1962-63** Yorkshire **1963-64** Cumberland **1964-65** Yorkshire **1965-66** Cumberland
1966-67 Cumberland **1967-68** Lancashire **1968-69** Yorkshire **1969-70** Lancashire
1970-71 Yorkshire **1971-72** Yorkshire **1972-73** Yorkshire **1973-74** Lancashire **1974-75** Lancashire
1975-76 Yorkshire **1976-77** Yorkshire **1977-78** No competition **1978-79** Lancashire **1979-80** Lancashire
1980-81 Cumbria **1981-82** Cumbria **1982-83** Yorkshire

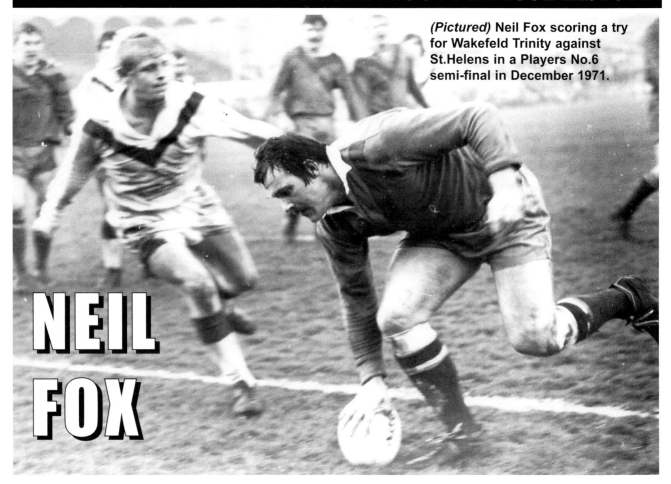

(Pictured) Neil Fox scoring a try for Wakefeld Trinity against St.Helens in a Players No.6 semi-final in December 1971.

NEIL FOX

THERE was a time when young Rugby League fans would eagerly open their *Football Final* newspapers on Saturday evenings to read an update of the list of the game's top try-scorers, goal-kickers and overall points scorers. Those vital statistics were always a massive part of the game and the players involved - as they were the men with their names in the papers more than any others - achieved superstar status.

Rugby League is different now. The absence of Saturday afternoon games had made those *Football Finals* redundant and with the inflated scorelines of the modern game the mystique about breaking points scoring records has been diminished. Neil Fox still proudly stands top of the list of all-time points scorers in the history of the game, with the general assumption being that nobody will ever overtake his grand total of 6,220 points as long as Rugby League is played.

But, there was a time, no doubt, when exactly the same would be said about Jim Sullivan's mammoth total of 6,022 points. It seemed inconceivable that anybody could ever get near that, and then along came Neil Fox. He started his senior career with Wakefield Trinity as a 16-year-old in an away match against Keighley at Lawkholme

Lane in April 1956, and he called "time" on his professional career 23 years later after playing for Bradford Northern against Huddersfield at Fartown in August 1979.

As well as Bradford, Neil also played for Hull K.R., York and Bramley, but his name will always be synonymous with Wakefield Trinity. "My heart was always at Wakefield," Neil has confirmed. "The club will always be very special to me and I was particularly proud to be associated with that great Trinity team of the early 'sixties."

A legend in Wakefield, and an icon throughout the Rugby League, Neil Fox was always respected as a gentleman as well as a great footballer. His career record of 6,220 points in senior football should stand forever.

TOP TEN POINTS SCORERS OF ALL TIME

6.220 NEIL FOX (Wakefield, Bradford, Hull K.R., York, Bramley, Huddersfield) *1956-1979.*

6,022 JIM SULLIVAN (Wigan) *1921-1946.*

4,050 GUS RISMAN (Salford, Workington, Batley) *1929-1954.*

3,985 JOHN WOODS (Leigh, Bradford, Warrington, Rochdale) *1976-1992.*

3,686 CYRIL KELLETT (Hull K.R., Featherstone) *1956-1974.*

3,545 KEL COSLETT (St.Helens), Rochdale) *1962-1979.*

3,445 LEWIS JONES (Leeds) *1952-1964.*

3,438 STEVE QUINN (York, Featherstone) *1970-1988.*

3,279 JIMMY LEDGARD (Leeds, Dewsbury, Leigh) *1944-1961.*

3,117 DAVID WATKINS (Salford, Swinton, Cardiff City) *1967-1982.*

Step into the Rugby League
TIME TUNNEL

The following section of this Annual presents our Club Nostalgia pages with memories of all your favourite clubs of old ... followed by a Walk Down Memory Lane as we remember days gone by in Rugby League.

SAVONNE

JIMENEZ

MERQUEY

BENAUSSE

QUAGLIO

FAGES

TONUS

PANO

IRVINE

JEAN BARTHE

This picture is from a Test match between France and Australia at the Parc des Princes, Paris in 1959. Ken Irvine is the solitary Kangaroo facing up to nine Frenchmen led by Jean Barthe.

(Above) Peter Douglas, a very talented Barrow stand-off in the 1960s, pictured in action at Whitehaven, with the Cumbrians' Bill Martin and John Shimmings on defence. Peter Douglas was signed by St.Helens and was one of several fine players to move from Barrow to Knowsley Road, among them Tommy Bishop, in later years Les Quirk and Tony Kay, and in the Super League era, Ade Gardner.

(Above) Eddie Szymala - one of Barrow's most popular players in the 1970s and '80s - tough, uncompromising, Eddie wasn't nicknamed "Smiler" for nothing. He represented both England and Great Britain.

> at Craven Park
>
> **B A R R O W**
>
> SATURDAY, 3ʀᴰ FEB., 1968
> R. L. CHALLENGE CUP - 1ˢᵀ ROUND
> KICK-OFF 3-0 p.m.
> VERSUS   2440
>
> **WAKEFIELD T.**
>
> By kind permission of N.W. Evening Mail
>
> **R F C**   6ᴰ

Wembley-bound in 1967, forty years on the faces of this Barrow team *(above)* remain very familiar. Left to right, *(Standing):* Mick Watson, Mike Sanderson, Ray Hopwood, Henry Delooze, Terry Kirchin, Brian Backhouse, Mike Murray, Maurice Redhead. *(Seated):* Bill Burgess, Eddie Tees, Ivor Kelland, Jim Challinor (captain-coach), Harry Hughes, Ged Smith and Bob Wear. They lost narrowly 17-12 to Featherstone Rovers and remain the last Barrow team to go to Wembley - it was the club's fifth appearance there in a Challenge Cup Final, a proud record which included three Wembleys in six years in the 1950s.

QUIZ

Question: Who were the two captains of Barrow when they won the Lancashire Cup, in 1954 and in 1983?

Eddie Tees - Barrow full-back at Wembley in 1967, followed the Willie Horne style as a side-footer.

(Right) John Carroll is pictured in possession for Batley in the 1980s. Carroll was a tough and talented second-rower who first made a big impression in the professional ranks with Leeds. After making a strong comeback from a broken leg, he joined Batley and enjoyed some good seasons at Mount Pleasant. Later he played for Heavy Woollen neighbours Dewsbury.

(Above) Paul Storey was one of the finest servants the Batley club has had throughout the long history of the "Gallant Youths." As one of the best full-backs they've had at Mount Pleasant (and they've seen some good 'uns, like Charlie Eaton, Peter Bateson and Stan Gittins) Storey had a long playing career before emerging as an equally talented coach. He learned his rugby with the Batley Boys junior club - a prolific nursery for producing professional players - and always stuck by the motto he was told by Director George Harwood who signed him for Batley: *"There's no better feeling than when you are playing for your home town."* Paul's talents were more widely recognised when he was included in the Great Britain training squad in 1986.

Batley CA & FC LTD.

THE GALLANT YOUTHS

OFFICIAL PROGRAMME 5p

QUIZ
Question: Who was the last Batley player to win Test selection for Great Britain?

Memories at the Mount.

Pictured (left) the Batley team in 1954 contained some of the best players of the post-War years at Mount Pleasant, among them back-line stars Bill Riches, John Etty and Sam Calvert, plus international forward George Palmer. The team is, left to right, (Standing): Bill Riches, John Etty, Jim Etty, Frank Mawson, Bob Kavanagh, Ken Pickersgill, George Palmer. (In front): Jonty Pilkington, H.McIntyre, William Leake, Newman, Gus Steele and Sam Calvert. Most of this Batley team had won through to the Yorkshire Cup Final in 1952.

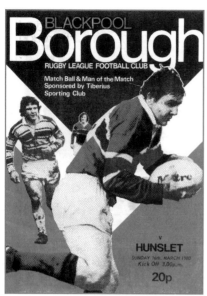

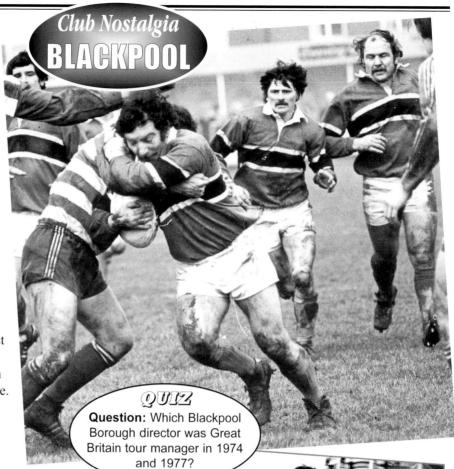

(Right) John Corcoran pictured in action for Blackpool Borough against Oldham in February 1981. Corcoran was a regular captain of the Borough in that era and always led by example.

(Above) Tommy Bishop, one of Blackpool's most famous products, receives the Borough player-of-the-year award for 1961 from the donor of the trophy, Mr. J. Kilkenny.

QUIZ

Question: Which Blackpool Borough director was Great Britain tour manager in 1974 and 1977?

(Right) Terry "Tex" McCarrick on his way to a try for Blackpool against Swinton at Borough Park in 1968. Tex was the full-back and goal-kicker for the Borough for six seasons between 1963 and 1969.

(Left) the traditional Blackpool team photograph carefully posed, as always, in front of the impressive grandstand at Borough Park. This was the Borough in the 1965-66 season, left to right: *(Standing):* Fred Hill, Frank Sullivan, Albert Seddon, John Fairhurst, Terry McCarrick, Alan Whitworth, Norman Ince, Brian Winstanley, Mick Ducie, Bob Rippon (kit-man), B. Watt (masseur.) *(Seated):* Brian Holmes, Ged Hall, Ken Large, Martin Dickens, Jimmy Gee and Alf Meakin.

113 **BRADFORD NORTHERN -**
RUGBY LEAGUE FOOTBALL CLUB
(1964) LTD.

ODSAL STADIUM . BRADFORD
SEASON 1964-65

Yorkshire County Cup - 1st Round
BRADFORD NORTHERN
versus
HUDDERSFIELD
SATURDAY, 5th SEPTEMBER, 1964
Kick-Off 3 p.m.

Official Programme Price 3d.

(Above) The Bradford Northern team at Odsal in the 1957-58 season. Left to right: *Standing):* Jones, Radford, Scroby, Hemingway, Kosanovic, Carter. *(In front):* Jenkins, Smith, L.Haley, Daniels, D.Davies, Oddy and M.Davies.

(Right) Ellery Hanley as a young player in the Bradford colours. Even in those early days at Odsal it was obvious that Ellery was destined to be a star, but nobody could have predicted the massive impact he was to have on the game. As Rugby League's first real professional player, he captained and coached Great Britain and became the biggest name in the game.

QUIZ

Question: Who captained Bradford Bulls when they won their first Super League title in 1997?

Bradford Northern in the 1973 Challenge Cup Final against Dewsbury as scrum-half Barry Seabourne gets a pass away from the scrum base as colleagues Dave Stockwell and Mike Lamb look on and Stan Fearnley is in support on the left.

JIM WINDSOR

Club Nostalgia

BRAMLEY

BRAMLEY *versus* **YORK**

OFFICIAL PROGRAMME 4p

Date Saturday, 26th August
Kick-off 3.00 p.m.
Venue McLAREN FIELD
NEXT HOME MATCH :
Tuesday, 29th August Kick-off 6.45 p.m.
Bramley versus Batley

(Above) Ray Price, Bramley hooker in the early 1970s.

(Above) Memories of the old Bramley ground, this action picture taken in 1952, with the well known Barley Mow Hotel in the background where the players used to get changed.
(Inset photo) Big Jim Windsor, Bramley's most generous supporter in the Barley Mow days.

QUIZ

Question: Who was Bramley's captain-coach when they won the BBC2 Floodlit Trophy in 1973?

Bramley in the late 1950s - left to right: *(Standing):* J.Wilson, G.Bloomfield, L.Hammill, J.Guy, A.Wood, D.Cranswick, G.Dooler, T.A.Smith. *(In front):* E.Humphreys, D.Kelly, W.Rushton, G. Langfield and G.Dudley.

(Below) Johnny Wolford, one of the true "greats" in the history of Bramley Rugby League club, pictured in action at McLaren Field during the 1972-73 season. He played a total of 683 games in a 23-year professional career which also took him to Bradford, Dewsbury and Hunslet.

Among the well known players on this team like Alf Wood, George Langfield, Geoff Dudley and Len Hammill (of Featherstone Rovers fame), none will be more synonymous with the Bramley club than full-back John Wilson. A Maori who came from Rugby Union in New Zealand to England to play League, first for a season at Dewsbury before moving across to the Barley Mow, he gave ten years magnificent service to "The Villagers" between 1953 and 1963. During that time he played almost 400 first team games and kicked 904 goals and was respected throughout the game as a rock solid custodian in the Bramley team. After hanging up his kicking boots, John stayed in the city of Leeds which had become his home and was a pub landlord for many years.

(Left) Malcolm Reilly playing for Cas' at Wembley in 1969 when they beat Salford to take the Cup and Malcolm won the Lance Todd trophy.

Castleford Rugby League Football Club Limited

Hon. Life President: Mr. Gideon Shaw
Directors:
Chairman - Mr. H. H. Clarkson
Mr. G. Shaw   Mr. A. E. Ellaby
Mr. A. E. Clarkson   Mr. B. Simpson   Mr. F. Smith   Mr. T. G. Harries
Hon. Club Doctor: Dr. A. B. C. Smith   Mr. F. L. Hartley   Mr. W. E. Brown
Secretary - Mr. L. Garbett

Castleford v. SWINTON
Saturday, 4th April, 1964   Kick-off 3.0 p.m.

Official Programme - Fourpence

SHAW, CASTLEFORD

(Above) Proud winners of the Yorkshire Cup in 1986, Castleford skipper John Joyner displays the famous old trophy alongside man-of-the-match, hooker Kevin Beardmore, holding the White Rose trophy. Castleford had just beaten Hull 31-24 at Headingley in the Final to win the Yorkshire Cup for the third time in their history.

The Castleford team of 1962 pictured at Wheldon Road.
Left to right: *(Standing):* Peter Small, John Berry, Bill Brownley, Geoff Ward, Johnny Walker, Bill Bryant, Johnny Ward.
(In front): Keith Hepworth, John Sheridan (Captain), Alan Hardisty, Albert Lunn, Brian Marsden and Colin Battye.

(Left) A familiar face in the world of Super League - but do any of the present-day fans recognise him from when he was Dewsbury's captain, inspiration and international star? Today he's "Stevo," but back in the early 1970s he was "Mick Stivvie" and Dewsbury's first Great Britain player for many years. The Bates brothers emulated him in 1974 but Stephenson remains Dewsbury's finest.

QUIZ

Question: Who was Dewsbury's famous manager during the World War Two years?

(Above) Paul Delaney a fine Dewsbury player in the 1990s.

(Above) Lionel Cooper is a famous name in Rugby League, always associated with Huddersfield, but the great Australian wingman also had a spell with Dewsbury as their trainer-coach. Lionel retired as a player at Fartown in 1955 and was appointed coach at Dewsbury in the 1956-57 season. The Dewsbury team group pictured is, left to right: *(Standing):* Lionel Cooper (Trainer-coach), C.Waterson, D.Cox, G.Popplewell, H.Grainger, D.Cawthra, J.Farrar, T.Danter. *(In front):* J.Curley, J.Clark, P.Todd (Captain), E.Lea, R.Taylor and F.Millican.

Dewsbury - the Rugby League Champions in 1972-73. Left to right: *(Standing):* Joe Whittington, John Clarke, Trevor Lowe, Jeff Grayshon, Harry Beverley, John Bates, Jeff Yoward, Adrian Rushton, B. Robinson. *(Seated):* Greg Ashcroft, Terry Day, Allan Agar, Mick Stephenson (Captain), Alan Bates, Nigel Stephenson and Steve Lee.

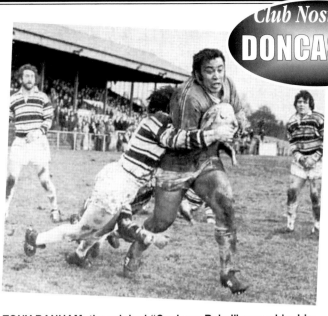

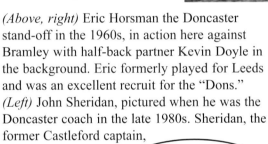

TONY BANHAM, the original "Cockney Rebel" was a big, big favourite with Doncaster supporters. Pictured here on his way to a typically barnstorming try for the Dons at Tattersfield against his former club Hull, Tony would have thrived in the modern game of unlimited substitutions as he was one of Rugby League's most lethal "impact" forwards.

(Above, right) Eric Horsman the Doncaster stand-off in the 1960s, in action here against Bramley with half-back partner Kevin Doyle in the background. Eric formerly played for Leeds and was an excellent recruit for the "Dons."

(Left) John Sheridan, pictured when he was the Doncaster coach in the late 1980s. Sheridan, the former Castleford captain, helped bring a big improvement at Tatters Field.

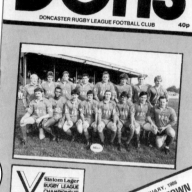

THE **DONS**
DONCASTER RUGBY LEAGUE FOOTBALL CLUB   40p

Slalom Lager RUGBY LEAGUE CHAMPIONSHIP DIVISION TWO

SUNDAY 12th JANUARY, 1986
WORKINGTON TOWN
K.O. 2.30pm

QUIZ
Question: Which future Doncaster coach was a Wembley winner with Barrow in 1955?

(Left) Doncaster in the 1972-73 season, a year in which they finsihed 27th in the 30-team Rugby League.
Left to right,
(Standing): Larry Lester, Tony Jeff, Malcolm Yates, Terry Lawrence, John Evans, Paul Carlin, Alan Goodyear.
(In front): Jimmy Banks, Pete Moody, David Elliott, Trevor Denton, Kennedy and Ken Rushton.

Featherstone Rovers pictured before playing York in a Cup tie at Clarence Street on 7th March 1959, a game which the Rovers won 18-7. Left to right: *(Standing):* Gary Cooper, Wynn Jones, Cyril Woolford, Joe Anderson, Frank Smith, Terry Clawson. *(Seated):* Alan Marchant, Jim Hunt, Willis Fawley, Joe Mullaney (Captain), Ken Greatorex, Mick Clamp and Norman Hockley.

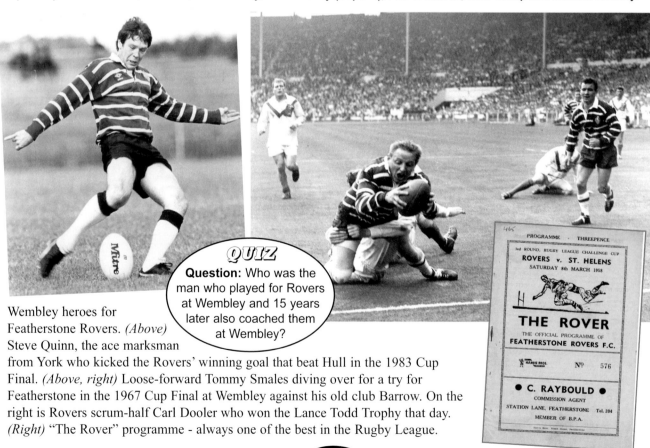

QUIZ

Question: Who was the man who played for Rovers at Wembley and 15 years later also coached them at Wembley?

Wembley heroes for Featherstone Rovers. *(Above)* Steve Quinn, the ace marksman from York who kicked the Rovers' winning goal that beat Hull in the 1983 Cup Final. *(Above, right)* Loose-forward Tommy Smales diving over for a try for Featherstone in the 1967 Cup Final at Wembley against his old club Barrow. On the right is Rovers scrum-half Carl Dooler who won the Lance Todd Trophy that day. *(Right)* "The Rover" programme - always one of the best in the Rugby League.

PROGRAMME · THREEPENCE

3rd ROUND, RUGBY LEAGUE CHALLENGE CUP

ROVERS v. ST. HELENS

SATURDAY 8th MARCH 1958

THE ROVER

THE OFFICIAL PROGRAMME OF
FEATHERSTONE ROVERS F.C.

HARRIS BROS.   Nº 576

● C. RAYBOULD ●
COMMISSION AGENT
STATION LANE, FEATHERSTONE   Tel. 204
MEMBER OF B.P.A.

52

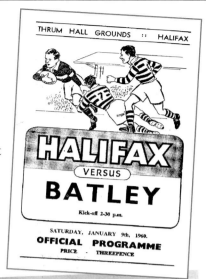

(Below) Halifax as winners of the Yorkshire Cup in the mid-'fifties captained by their Cumbrian hooker from Maryport Alvin Ackerley. He skippered Halifax to successive Yorkshire Cups in 1954 and 1955 - both Finals being won against Hull. That was in a great era for the team from Thrum Hall with a big and tough pack of forwards.

(Above) Barry Robinson on the attack for Halifax in the 1963 Yorkshire Cup Final against Featherstone Rovers. Robinson was a big favourite with the fans at Thrum Hall in a career that lasted 12 years from 1959 to 1971, after joining Halifax from the Shaw Cross club in Dewsbury. Filling the shoes of the great Ken Dean as stand-off in the blue and white hoops was a big challenge, but Barry did it well - his career highlight coming as half-back partner to Paul Daley in Halifax's 1965 Championship win.

QUIZ
Question: Who was Halifax's coach when they won the Rugby League Championship in 1964-65?

The Halifax team of 1971-72, a season in which they became the first winners of the "Players No. 6" trophy and also reached the semi-final of the Challenge Cup. They are, left to right: *(Standing):* Les Pearce (Coach), Terry Fogerty, Dave Callon, Phil Davies, Terry Dewhirst. Tony Hepworth, David Willicombe, Tony Halmshaw. *(In front):* John Martin, Roy Hawksley, Mike Kelly, Derek Reeves, Gordon Baker, John "Sammy" Sanderson, Dave Rayner and Bruce Burton.

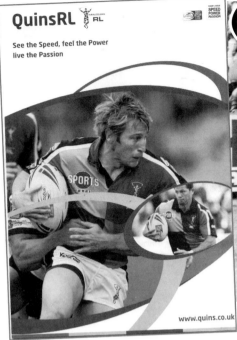

QuinsRL RL

See the Speed, feel the Power
live the Passion

www.quins.co.uk

(Above) Harlequins advertising in 2006 as they promote the new face of professional Rugby League in London - yet the bloodlines and fan loyalties of the new "brand" can be traced all the way back through the London Broncos and Crusaders to the original Fulham club.

Pictured *(right)* is a scene from the time Fulham were playing at Crystal Palace as the Cumbrian forward Harold Henney, who proved to be an enthusiastic recruit for the Londoners, leads them against Sheffield. And, just to emphasise those bloodlines, the Eagles player on the left is Paul McDermott, whose younger brother Brian became the new Harlequins coach in 2006.

(Above) Fulham heroes from the early Craven Cottage days as the prolific try-scorer John Crossley grabs another touchdown - this one against Wigan at Central Park with Hussein M'Barki in support.

QUIZ

Question: Who was Fulham's first player-coach and who did they beat in their first League game in 1980?

By the 1987-88 season, Fulham were playing at the old Polytechnic Stadium at Chiswick, and their battles for survival bred incredible loyalty from supporters. This is the Fulham team which played at York in April 1988 - among them Nick Grimoldby, Nicky Elgar, Dave Gillan and Russell Bridge.

(Top,left) Two Fartown stalwarts, Peter Ramsden and Tommy Smales, were the two Huddersfield try-scorers in the 1962 Challenge Cup Final which was lost 12-6 to Wakefield Trinity. *(Above)* Preparing for that trip to Wembley, the players take a break from training at Fartown to listen to coach Dave Valentine. They are, left to right: *(Standing):* Brian Rowe, Ken Bowman, Ken Noble, Ted Slevin, Eddie Strong, Peter Ramsden, Harry Deighton, Austin Kilroy, Don Close, Frank Dyson, Brian Curry. *(In front):* Geoff Stocks, Mr.Valentine, Tommy Smales and Mike Wicks.

QUIZ

Question: Who was the captain of Fartown's famous "Team of All Talents?"

The Huddersfield team at the start of the 1948-49 season with stars drawn from Scotland, Ireland, Wales, Cumberland and Australia. Left to right: *(Standing):* John Daly, Bob Nicholson, Bob Robson, Mel Meek, Lionel Cooper, Jack Maiden. *(In front):* Johnny Hunter, Jeff Bawden, Russ Pepperell, Stanley Walsh, Pat Devery (Captain), Paddy Reid and Dave Valentine.

These five gentlemen laid the platform for Hull's great successes of the second half of the 1950s. They were the feared Hull pack which included *(left to right):* Jim Drake, Mick Scott, Tommy Harris, Bill Drake and Johnny Whiteley. If the Drake brothers provided the hard edge, Harris and Whiteley put on footballing skills way ahead of their time. Their achievements included three consecutive Championship Finals (two won), followed by two Wembley Cup Finals.

(Above) "Sammy" Lloyd, a prolific goal-kicking second-rower for Hull in the successful years of the early 1980s, after signing from Castleford.

QUIZ

Question: Who captained Hull when they won the Challenge Cup in the Elland Road replay of 1982?

OFFICIAL PROGRAMME 6d.

HULL
R.L.F.C.

The Airlie Birds

VERSUS

WIGAN

SATURDAY, 26th SEPTEMBER, 1970

(Above) The Hull team in front of a crowd of 27,000 at the Boulevard for the Good Friday derby match with Hull K.R. in 1958 as the "Airlie Birds" were on their way to a top-four place and, ultimately, the Championship - beating Workington Town in the Final. Left to right: *(Standing):* Jim Drake, Brian Hambling, Geoff Dannatt, Bill Drake, Brian Cooper, Mick Scott, Peter Bateson. *(In front):* Brian Saville, Ivor Watts, Johnny Whiteley (Captain), Tommy Finn, Tommy Harris and Frank Broadhurst.

HULL KINGSTON ROVERS
VERSUS
WORKINGTON
NORTHERN RUGBY FOOTBALL LEAGUE—FIRST DIVISION
WEDNESDAY, 29th MAY, 1963
Craven Park, Hull
Kick-off 6-30 p.m.

EASTERN DIVISION CHAMPIONS
1962-1963

RALLY ROUND ROVERS

OFFICIAL PROGRAMME 4d.

Robins on tour with the Great Britain team in Australia in 1962, prop-forward John Taylor *(left)* and trainer-coach Colin Hutton. Taylor became the very first Hull K.R. player to be a Lions tourist.

(Above) Loose-forward Joe Brown playing for Hull K.R. in the 1974 Yorkshire Cup Final in which Rovers beat Wakefield 16-13.

(Right) Hull Kingston Rovers celebrate winning the 1984 Premiership, beating Castleford in the Final at Headingley. John Dorahy, on the left of the front row, is holding his award as the winner of the Harry Sunderland Trophy, while team-mates at the front: Chris Burton, John Millington, David Hall and Ian Robinson toast the Robins' victory.

QUIZ

Question: Which future Australian Test captain guested with Hull K.R. in 1968 before breaking his leg?

(Left) The Hull Kingston Rovers team in their dressing-room at Boothferry Park before going out to beat local rivals Hull F.C. 21-20 in a League match in October, 1955. The Robins had given up their "home" fixture to play at the Hull City soccer ground and were rewarded with a crowd of 16,670 and receipts of £1,911. The players are, left to right: *(Standing):* Keith Golding, Jim Shires, Arthur Garry, Ken Grice, Bernard Golder, Tom Sutton, Sam Evans, John Hall. *(In front):* Alan Bartliff, John Parker, Jim Tong (Captain), Terry Buckle and Maurice Thornton.

A reminder of those old Parkside days *(above)* as Hunslet winger Alan Snowden is pictured diving over at the corner in typical style for a try in a city derby against Bramley. Snowden was one of the finest wingers in the illustrious history of Hunslet - he signed for them from Roundhay Rugby Union and set a Hunslet record of 34 tries in a season (1956-57). In a total of 213 games for the club he scored 151 tries, before being transferred to Halifax in 1958 where he also became a big favourite with the Thrum Hall fans.

QUIZ
Question: Which Hunslet icon captained them in their last ever match to be played at the old Parkside ground?

(Above) The Hunslet team of 1987 celebrate winning the Championship of the Second Division. In the centre of the group is their captain Terry Webb, arms aloft, being carried on the shoulders of coach David Ward and manager Peter Jarvis.

THE PARKSIDER
PRICE 3d.
SECRETARY—H. Jepson
SAT. JANUARY 18th, 1964
TELEPHONE 76444
879

SCRAP METALS, FERROUS & NON-FERROUS BUYERS
IF YOU WANT IT - *we have it*
IF YOU DON'T - *we'll buy it*
RING 77895
JOHN JARRETT LTD.
GOODMAN STREET, LEEDS, 10

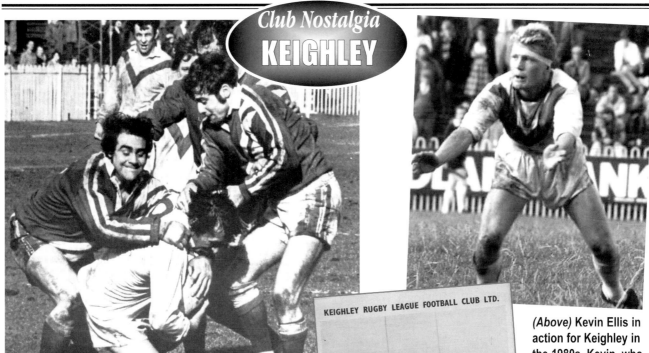

(Above) The Challenge Cup semi-final in 1976 and Keighley went within a solitary point of going to Wembley, going down 5-4 to the eventual Cup winners St.Helens. The picture shows Keighley forward Tony Garforth and full-back Brian Jefferson bringing a Saints player to ground in a match in which the boys from Lawkholme Lane scared the life out of the hot favourites from St.Helens. Had they won, it would have been Keighley's second visit to Wembley after they lost there to Widnes in the 1937 Cup Final.

KEIGHLEY RUGBY LEAGUE FOOTBALL CLUB LTD.

Ground: LAWKHOLME LANE   **3d.**

KEIGHLEY v. OLDHAM 1993

SATURDAY, FEBRUARY 8th, 1964   KICK-OFF 3-0 p.m.

Phone: Bingley 3345

THE KEIGHLEY R.L.F.C. TEAMS TRAVEL BY

WARDWAYS LIMITED.

MAIN STREET, BINGLEY

For your next outing consult us. Luxury Coaches available for Private Parties.
Agent:—H. MOORE, 21/23, BRIDGE STREET, KEIGHLEY. Phone: 4674

"CALLING ALL SUPPORTERS"
WANTED!
A FEW MORE COLLECTORS FOR OUR
DAILY DRAW
TO INCREASE THE PRIZE MONEY TO £50 PER D
IT COULD BE YOUR LUCKY SEASON — 14 CASH PRIZES EA
Particulars from the Promoter :— Malcolm Davies, 18b, Spen

(Above) Kevin Ellis in action for Keighley in the 1980s. Kevin, who played in both half-back positions, not only was a useful footballer but he also did a lot of excellent work to help promote the club at Lawkholme Lane in those difficult pre-Cougar days.

QUIZ

Question: Which former Keighley player is now a coach of the French Rugby Union team?

Keighley in the 1962-63 season when they won promotion to the First Division of the Rugby League after a very successful campaign. Left t right, *(Standing):* Jack Taylor (physio), Billy Watson (kitman), Harry Plunkett, Albert Eyre, Barry Anderson, Vince Jackson, Geoff Crewdson, Kenny Pye, Frank Haigh, Gordon Brown (coach.) *(In front):* Alfie Barron, Bryan Todd, Roy Bleasby, Garfield Owen, Terry Jackson and Roy Sabine. The coach at Lawkholme Lane that year, Gordon Brown, had been one of Great Britain's heroes in the first World Cup in 1954 when he was a young player with Leeds.

Leeds in the spring of 1972, the days when duffle-coats ruled and the Loiners were on their way to Wembley. The players are, left to right, *(Standing):* Phil Cookson, John Holmes, David Ward, Terry Clawson, Ray Batten, Bill Ramsey, Fred Pickup, Graham Eccles, David Hick. *(In front):* Keith Hepworth, Alan Smith, Alan Hardisty, Syd Hynes, John Langley and John Atkinson.

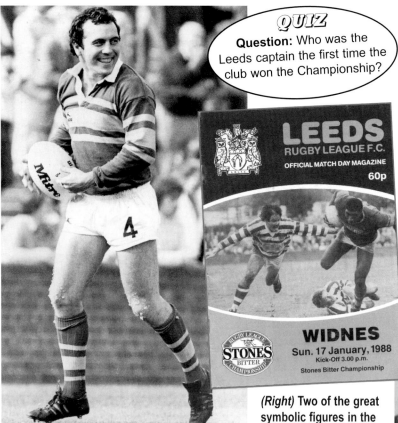

QUIZ

Question: Who was the Leeds captain the first time the club won the Championship?

LEEDS
RUGBY LEAGUE F.C.
OFFICIAL MATCH DAY MAGAZINE
60p

WIDNES
Sun. 17 January, 1988
Kick-Off 3.00 p.m.
Stones Bitter Championship

(Right) Barry Simms, the Leeds hooker and a key player in their first Championship title winning season in 1960-61. Simms also got to play a solitary Test for Great Britain versus France in 1962.

(Above) Les Dyl - a man who always played the game with a smile on his face and was very popular with Leeds fans and throughout the game. His centre/wing partnership with John Atkinson was a special combination for the Loiners.

(Right) Two of the great symbolic figures in the Leeds glory years - as the charismatic coach Roy Francis enjoys his taste for champagne to help celebrate the 1968 Wembley win with stand-off Mick Shoebottom.

QUIZ

Question: Who was the Leigh full-back who played in Great Britain's first World Cup winning team in 1954?

(Above) Anxious looks from the Leigh pack during a tense moment in a Challenge Cup tie at Featherstone in 1962 - among the Leigh forwards are Mick Martyn and Stan Owen. It was a game Leigh lost 23-9 to the Rovers at Post Office Road in front of a crowd in excess of 11,000.

(Above) **Steve Donlan, a very skilful footballer in Leigh's Champions team of 1982. Steve was a Lions tourist in 1984 and also captained England.**

Leigh Football Club Ltd.

Headquarters: Hilton Park

A. & B. Motors Cup

LEIGH v. WIDNES

Saturday, 12th August, 1967
Kick-Off 3.00 p.m.

Official Programme

6D.

Nº 1199

(Above) Leigh, the Rugby League Champions in the 1981-82 season, one of the greatest achievements in their long history. The team are, left to right:*(Back row):* Tommy Martyn, Ian Potter, Tony Cooke, Alf Wilkinson, Mick Stacey, S.Tomlinson. *(Middle row):* Ken Green, Ray Tabern, Derek Pyke, Roy Howarth, Mick McTigue, Phil Fox, Terry Bilsbury. *(Front row):*Bill Kindon (Trainer), David Dunn, Mick Hogan, John Woods (Captain), Des Drummond, Steve Donlan, Alex Muphy (Coach).

(Above) **Colin Tyrer, one of the best goal-kickers to be produced in Leigh. Won Great Britain Under-24 honours whilst at Hilton Park before moving on to Wigan.**

OLDHAM RUGBY LEAGUE FOOTBALL CLUB

RUGBY FOOTBALL LEAGUE
Northern League Championship Match
OLDHAM
v.
LIVERPOOL CITY
TUESDAY, 15th AUGUST, 1967
Kick-off 7.30 p.m.

OFFICIAL PROGRAMME 6d

(Above) Oldham gave the Kangaroos a real run for their money on the 1986 tour - as Hussein M'Barki gives chase to Aussies Greg Alexander and Mal Meninga at Watersheddings. Oldham held the Australians to 22-16, the closest margin by any club on the 1986 tour.

QUIZ

Question: Name the two former Oldham players who became assistant coaches of the England Rugby Union team?

(Above) Oldham boys on international duty - Des Foy and Terry Flanagan playing for the Great Brtain Under-24s in France in 1983. Terry is currently the chairman of his old amateur club, Saddleworth Rangers.

Threequarter-line stars of the Oldham Championship winning team of 1957 - Dennis Ayres *(top)* and John Etty *(above.)*

(Above) Didn't they look great when they looked like Oldham!! Instantly recognisable in the red and white hoops and navy blue shorts, the *Roughyeds* were one of the classiest teams in the Rugby League in the mid-fifties. The players in this team, captained by full-back Bernard Ganley, include: Roger Dufty, Derek Turner, Charlie Winslade, Jack Keith, Alan Kellett, John Etty, Johnny Noon, Alan Davies and Dick Cracknell. They formed the bulk of the classic Oldham side which won the Rugby League Championship in 1957, and three successive Lancashire Cups. Sadly for them, and the game as a whole, they never got to play at Wembley - along with Swinton, quite probably the best team never to grace the famous Twin Towers.

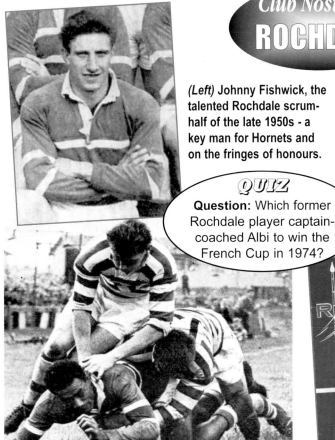

(Left) Johnny Fishwick, the talented Rochdale scrum-half of the late 1950s - a key man for Hornets and on the fringes of honours.

QUIZ

Question: Which former Rochdale player captain-coached Albi to win the French Cup in 1974?

(Above) Pictured as a young player in action for Rochdale is one of the Hornets' most successful products, Neil Cowie, who went on to win many winners' medals and international honours as a front-row-forward with the all-conquering Wigan team of the early 1990s. The other Rochdale Hornets players in the picture are Neil Lowe and Dean Williams.

(Above) Laitia Ravouvou - one of the popular Fijians who came to Rochdale in the 1960s - brought down by Wigan defenders as Hornets met them at the Athletic Grounds.

ROCHDALE
HORNETS
RUGBY LEAGUE
FOOTBALL CLUB

RUGBY FOOTBALL LEAGUE
ROCHDALE HORNETS
v.
WIDNES   6d.
SATURDAY, 31st OCTOBER, 1964
KICK-OFF 3.0 p.m.

The Rochdale Hornets team which went very close to a dramatic win against Wigan at Central Park in November 1968, losing by 17 points to 16. They are, left to right: *(Standing):* Michael Goddard, Dennis Murray, Henry Delooze, Michael Crocker, Eddie Brown, Peter Birchall, Mick Mooney, Joe Chamberlain, Jimmy Gaskell.
(In front): Tom Pimblett, Ian Entwistle, Ken Tighe, Graham Starkey (Captain), Norman Brelsford and Eddie Tees.

(Above) Salford in the early 1980s playing against Hull, with their international forward Mike Coulman in possession. Offering support to Mike are scrum-half Steve Nash and hooker Paul O'Neill.

(Above) Red Devils return - Salford greats Gus Risman and Emlyn Jenkins pictured in France in 1984 as Salford made a nostalgic return to Perpignan to play the X111 Catalan 50 years after Gus led the original Red Devils tour.

QUIZ
Question: Who was the influential club Chairman who built the star Salford teams of the 1970s?

Salford stars of the 'seventies - *(above)* Keith Fielding, the flying winger who became a dual-code international and *(below)* Paul Charlton, one of the finest full-backs the game has seen, signed by the Red Devils from Workington he won 19 Great Britain caps.

Salford of half a century ago - these were the "Red Devils" in the 1956-57 season. Left to right:*(Standing):* Hugh Duffy, Eric Ayles, Frank Alder, Frank Boardman, Derek Fieldhouse, John Cheshire, Peter Cordwell. *(In front):* Fred Smith, Arthur Gregory, Frank Dodd, Brian Keavney, Dai Moses and Ron Walker.

(Above) Memories of Sheffield Eagles' very first match in the Rugby League in 1984, versus Rochdale Hornets at the Owlerton Stadium. This picture from that game shows Eagles' stand-off Steve Robinson diving over to score a try.

(Left) David Mycoe, was a very important signing for the Eagles when he joined them in 1989 as a 17-year-old. The fact that he chose Sheffield ahead of several other clubs gave the Eagles a lot of new credibility.

Slalom Lager
SECOND DIVISION CHAMPIONSHIP
40p
THE SHEFFIELD EAGLES
V
17th APRIL 1985 KICK OFF 6.30 p.m.
KEIGHLEY
SPONSORED BY STONES BREWERY

QUIZ
Question: Who won the Lance Todd trophy when Sheffield won at Wembley in the 1998 Final?

(Above) The greatest moment in the life of Sheffield Eagles, as the final whistle went at Wembley in 1998 and they had beaten Wigan to win the Challenge Cup. Eagles Paul Broadbent and Michael Jackson jump for joy along with most of the crowd.

Expecting to fly ... these were the very first group of Sheffield Eagles, pictured in training in the lead up to the club's debut in the Rugby League in 1984. Among those pictured are the club's first coach and conditioner, Alan Rhodes and Stan Timmins, on the back row with players inclduing Billy Harris, Dave Alred (better known now as the Rugby Union's kicking-guru) and Vince Farrar - whilst in front there's a very young Daryl Powell, the club founder Gary Hetherington, Ray Smith and Paul McDermott.

QUIZ

Question: Which Saints player won the Lance Todd Trophy when they won at Wembley in 1961?

Saints have played in plenty of Cup Finals so they know all about the pressures of winning semi-finals. *(Above)* winger Les Quirk is congratulated by David Tanner after a scoring try in the 1989 semi against Widnes.

(Above) Mal Meninga lifts the Premiership trophy for St.Helens in 1985. Big Mal made a massive impression in his year with the Saints.

(Left) Hero worship - and nobody has been a bigger hero to the fans in the story of St.Helens than the South African flyer Tom Van Vollenhoven. In this picture of early days at Knowsley Road, Tom signs autographs still sporting his Springbok blazer and tie. Tom made another very nostalgic visit to England in 2006 and had the honour of leading the modern day Saints out at the Challenge Cup Final.

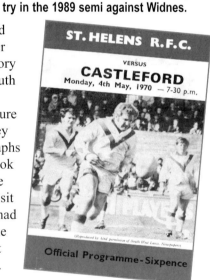

ST. HELENS R.F.C.

VERSUS

CASTLEFORD
Monday, 4th May, 1970 — 7-30 p.m.

(Reproduced by kind permission of South West Lancs. Newspapers)

Official Programme - Sixpence

(Left) The Saints in the 1958-59 season, a year in which they went on to win the Championship in spectacular style.
Left to right: *(Standing):* Vince Karalius, Abe Terry, Tom Van Vollenhovem Jan Prinsloo, Peter Fearis, E.Bowden, Brian Briggs, Dick Huddart. *(In front):* Dennis Karalius, Glyn Moses, Doug Greenall, Alex Murphy and Brian Howard. Missing from this line-up was skipper Alan Prescott.

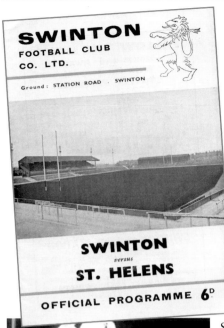

SWINTON
FOOTBALL CLUB
CO. LTD.

Ground: STATION ROAD · SWINTON

SWINTON
versus
ST. HELENS

OFFICIAL PROGRAMME 6ᴰ

Swinton greats from the team which won back-to-back Championships in the early 1960s *(above)* winger John Stopford and *(right)* full-back Ken Gowers. Both represented the "other" Lions on the 1966 tour of Australasia.

(Left) Les Holliday as he captained Swinton to the Second Division Premiership title at Old Trafford in 1987. Les followed in the footsteps of his father Bill Holliday in giving fine service to the Swinton club, and both father and son played for Great Britain.

QUIZ

Question: Who captained Swinton to their consecutive Championship titles in 1962-63 and 1963-64?

Swinton at Station Road in 1975

Left to right, *(Standing):* Lawrence Lowe, Graham Evans, John Cooke, Kevin Whittle, Mick Henighan, Jeff Whiteside, Tom Young, Bill Pattinson. *(Seated):* Les Bolton, John Houghton, Bob Fleet, Bob Fleay, Ken Green and Les Atkinson.

Read all about it in the *"Wakefield Express"* - these Trinity stars knew they were the men making the headlines in the swinging sixties in the "Merrie City." Left to right: Neil Fox, coach Ken Traill, Harold Poynton and captain Derek Turner.

(Above) Flashback to 1962 and the Trinity fullback Gerry Round in action against Leeds. Gerry joined Wakefield from the Hebden Bridge Amateur club and played in all three of their famous Wembley wins of the early '60s and was in the Ashes winning team of 1962. Tragically, he was killed in a car crash.

WAKEFIELD TRINITY
FOOTBALL CLUB

Official Programme - Sixpence

QUIZ

Question: Who was the Olympic sprinter who joined Wakefield, first playing trials under the name "Walker?"

(Right) Wakefield Trinity enjoy the moment they lifted the Challenge Cup at Wembley in 1962 after beating Huddersfield 12-6 in the Final. Skipper Derek Turner is carried aloft with the famous old trophy. The players are, left to right: *(Standing at the back):* Fred Smith, Dennis Williamson, Brian Briggs, Neil Fox, Jack Wilkinson, Keith Holliday, Gerry Round and Paddy Armour the masseur.
(In front): Harold Poynton, Alan Skene, Albert Firth, Ken Hirst and Geoff Oakes. In that Cup Final Neil Fox was awarded the Lance Todd Trophy after a top performance which included scoring a try after a 75-yard move and kicking three drop-goals - creating the six-point margin over a gallant Fartown.

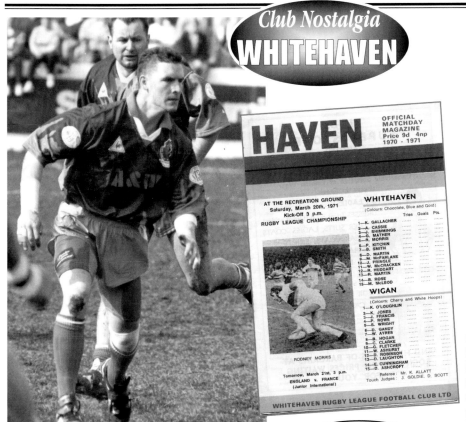

(Above) Bill Holliday in action for Whitehaven against Wigan in early 1965 - he went on to captain Great Britain in the 1967 Ashes.

(Right) in his trademark beret in 1956, former Wallaby Neville Emery was one of the most revered coaches in Whitehaven's history.

(Above) modern day "greats" of Whitehaven, David Seeds and Billy Fisher. Seeds the top try-scorer in the club's history, and Fisher second only to John McKeown in appearances.

QUIZ

Question: Who is the only current Whitehaven player to be included in the club's "Immortals" team?

The Whitehaven team pictured a couple of nights after they had beaten Wigan in a replay of the first round of the Top-16 play-off in 1970 and were preparing to travel to Headingley to play Leeds in the Championship quarter-final. They are, left to right: *(Standing):* Keith Hunter, Michael McFaralane, John Pringle, Sol Roper (Captain-coach), Harry Maddison, Tom Gainford, Bobby Ryan, Hedley Rogers (Trainer). *(Seated):* Barry Buchanan, John Shimmings, Ron Barnes, Billy McCracken, Peter Donnelly, Jim Powe, Gordon Cottier. *(Kneeling in front):* Dennis Martin, Raymond Martin, Mike Gracey and Matt McLeod.

Club Nostalgia
WARRINGTON

(Above) Warrington in the early 1960s as stand-off Jackie Edwards beats the Hull full-back Arthur Keegan to stretch over for a try - Wire's Test full-back Eric Fraser is the man in support.

WARRINGTON
RUGBY LEAGUE FOOTBALL CLUB

OFFICIAL
6d.
PROGRAMME
NOW **3p**

RUGBY FOOTBALL LEAGUE
(Northern League Championship Match)
WARRINGTON
v.
WHITEHAVEN
FRIDAY, APRIL 2nd, 1971
Kick-off 7.00 p.m.

(Above) The moment of glory for Warrington as player-coach Alex Murphy and his first lieutenant Kevin Ashcroft jump for joy as the Challenge Cup was won at Wembley in 1974. It was the last time the boys in primrose and blue lifted the Cup and was the highpoint of Murphy's successful reign as coach at Wilderspool after arriving from Leigh.

QUIZ
Question: Who was the New Zealander who managed Warrington to many triumphs in the 1950s?

Pictured at Wilderspool in the very early 1980s, how many of the youthful faces can you recognise on this Warrington team? On the back row they include: John Fieldhouse, Ronnie Duane, Bob Eccles, Steve Hesford, Neil Courtney, Tommy Martyn and Eddie Hunter, whilst on the front row there's Ken Kelly, John Bevan, Mike Kelly and Phil Ford. *(Photo by Eddie Whitham.)*

(Above) Wire captain Billy Benyon exchanges greetings and a pennant with Australian skipper Bob Fulton before Warrington became one of the last club teams to beat a Kangaroo touring side at Wilderspool in 1978. Fulton himself was born in Warrington before his family emigrated, and played as a guest for the club in the 1969-70 season. *(Photo by Eddie Whitham.)*

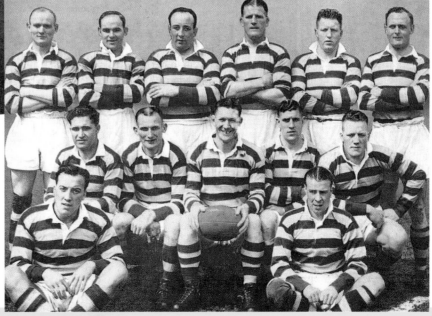

Grainy old images but unique, never seen before in colour from the days when black and white pictures were the only ones we saw. *(Above)* The legendary Brian Bevan on his way to a try against Blackpool Borough. *(Right)* The first Warrington Championship winning team, of 1947-48, captained by Harold Palin.

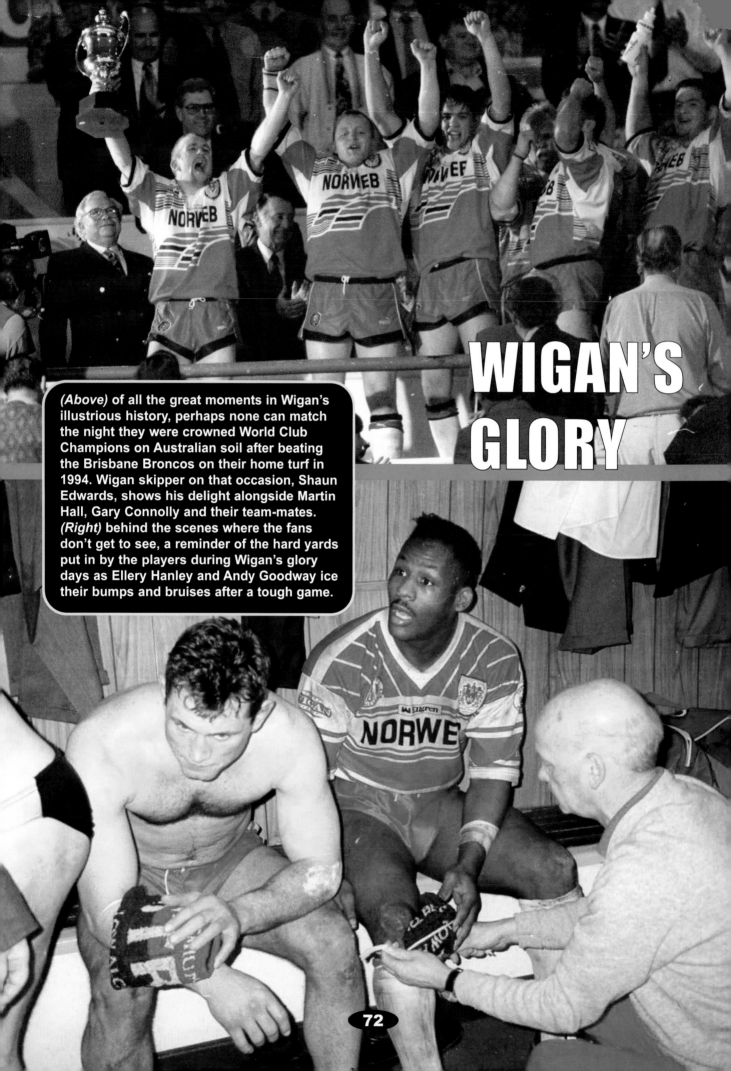

WIGAN'S GLORY

(Above) of all the great moments in Wigan's illustrious history, perhaps none can match the night they were crowned World Club Champions on Australian soil after beating the Brisbane Broncos on their home turf in 1994. Wigan skipper on that occasion, Shaun Edwards, shows his delight alongside Martin Hall, Gary Connolly and their team-mates.
(Right) behind the scenes where the fans don't get to see, a reminder of the hard yards put in by the players during Wigan's glory days as Ellery Hanley and Andy Goodway ice their bumps and bruises after a tough game.

QUIZ

Question: Who was the first Wigan-born player to captain a Great Britain Lions touring team to Australia?

NORTHERN RUGBY FOOTBALL LEAGUE

WIGAN
Nº 507 VERSUS

BLACKPOOL BOROUGH

Photograph by kind permission of Evening Post and Chronicle

OFFICIAL PROGRAMME Price 4d.

(Above) Roy Evans, loose-forward for Wigan in the late '50s and early '60s, a Wembley winner and Great Britain Test player, later gave fine service to the Blackpool Borough club.

(Above) Joe Egan, one of the all-time greats of Wigan and Great Britain, was the captain at Central Park in the early post-War years. *(Above, right)* Aussie stars Brett Kenny and John Ferguson - they only played in the cherry and white for a few months in 1984-85, but they left an unforgetable impression on the history of the Wigan club.

The Wigan team in 1962-63 season.
Left to right: *(Back row):* Tom Woosey, Jim Belshaw, David Bolton. *(Middle row):* Trevor Lake, Bill Sayer, Geoff Lyon, Roy Evans, Frank Collier. *(Front row):* Frank Carlton, Stan McLeod, Eric Ashton (Captain), Frank Pitchford and Alan Davies. *(Inset photos:* John Barton, Brian McTigue and Billy Boston. It was a season when Wigan were beaten finalists at Wembley.

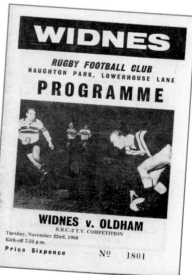

(Above) **Mick Adams with Keith Elwell in support - two local Widnes lads who were the dynamos of the Chemics' team in their remarkable run of successes through the 1970s and early '80s. Both also played for Lancashire, England and Great Britain.**

QUIZ
Question:
A Widnesian was the last man to captain Great Britain to the Ashes. Can you name him?

(Above) Widnes at Wembley in 1964 and the picture shows Jim Measures bringing down a Hull Kingston Rovers opponent as the Chemics won the Cup, captained by Vince Karalius. Measures was a really good second-row-forward who was a big part of that Widnes team and respected throughout the Rugby League. He played Test football alongside Karalius in the 1963 Ashes series against Australia.

(Above) **The Chemics in the 1961-62 season. Left to right:** *(Standing)*: **Bob Chisnall, Jim Bright, Ron Bate, Brian Keavney, Winstanley, Edgar Bate, Tom Smith.** *(In front)*: **Willie Thompson, Pimblett, Frank Myler, Harry Dawson, Smart and Major.**

WIDNES
RUGBY FOOTBALL CLUB
NAUGHTON PARK, LOWERHOUSE LANE
PROGRAMME

WIDNES v. OLDHAM
B.B.C-2 T.V. COMPETITION
Tuesday, November 22nd, 1966
Kick-off 7-25 p.m.
Price Sixpence   No 1801

Club Nostalgia
WORKINGTON

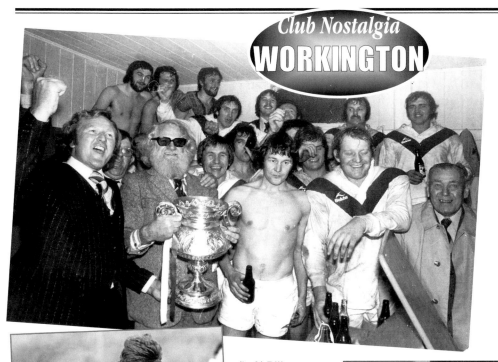

(Left) Workington Town, winners of the Lancashire Cup in 1977, enjoy happy dressing-room scenes after taking the trophy for the first time, led by senior players at the front: Paul Charlton (Captain), Iain McCorquadale and Les Gorley. Town officials on the picture include George Graham on the left and the inimitable Tom Mitchell holding the Cup. On the right is Jimmy Hodgson, a major figure in the history of the Workington club and, as "J.J.H.," an inspiration to all budding programme notes writers.

(Left) Billy Pattinson, one of the most loyal and energtic forwards to wear the Town colours. He represented England in 1981 and gave over a decade of service at Derwent Park.

QUIZ

Question: Can you name three former Lions touring team captains who later coached Workington Town?

(Above) Workington Town's three tourists with the Great Britain team in Australia in 1962 - Norman Herbert, Brian Edgar and Ike Southward. Edgar went on to join the select band of players who made three Lions tours.

When Workington Town were a strong force at the top level of the Rugby League, this team in 1963 pictured ready to take on Leeds at Headingley. Left to right: *(Standing):* Ike Southward, Walter Tabern, Brian Edgar, Matt McLeod, Bill Martin, Frank Foster. *(In front):* Eric Bell, John McFarlane, Sol Roper, Syd Lowden (Captain), Ray Glastonbury, Harry Hughes and Billy Smith.

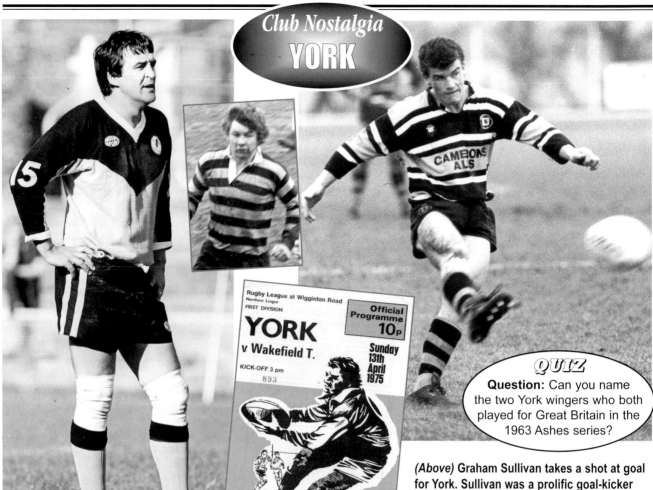

Rugby League at Wigginton Road
Northern League
FIRST DIVISION

YORK
v Wakefield T.

KICK-OFF 3 pm
893

Official
Programme
10p

Sunday
13th
April
1975

(Above) Graham Sullivan takes a shot at goal for York. Sullivan was a prolific goal-kicker and points scorer in the late 1980s and early '90s - the era when the club was known as Ryedale-York

(Inset - above, left) Richard Wallace in action for York in the 1970s. Wallace was an excellent utility back who originated from the West Country, first joining Huddersfield from Bristol Rugby Union club before moving east to Clarence Street and the Minster city.

(Above) Bill Kirkbride as a York player in the early 1980s. Bill, who came from Workington before winning the Lance Todd Trophy with Castleford in 1970, also had a spell as coach for the "Wasps" at Clarence Street. He coached Wakefield Trinity to Wembley in 1979.

(Left) Memories of York in the late 1950s - this team includes three of the best known "Yorkies" who gave such sterling service to their local club: Basil Watts, Vic Yorke and Stan Flannery. Also at the front is the long-serving full-back Willie Hargreaves. Basil Watts was a member of Great Britain's heroic team which won the very first World Cup.

Down Memory Lane

To remember the way we were

(Above) One of those incidents where the presence of a "video referee" would have changed the destiny of a Cup Final and the game's history. This flashback is to the 1957 Challenge Cup Final at Wembley and Leeds full-back Pat Quinn has just been awarded the opening try for the Loiners in what

proved to be a narrow 9-7 win over Barrow. But had Quinn dropped the ball as he crossed the line near the corner flag? Barrow winger Jimmy Lewthwaite was one of sport's great gentlemen and would never have appealed as the picture shows if he had not genuinely believed it was "no try."

(Left) Reading all about it the paper - a scene from the Olympic Hotel in Sydney during the 1962 Lions tour as Great Britain stars Billy Boston and Alex Murphy check out what the Australian press was saying about them. With Boston and Murphy is the Lions tour manager Mr. Stuart Hadfield from the Wakefield Trinity club. Billy Boston had been one of six players (including all four wingers) sent off in the tourists' match against New South Wales, and he was taking a look at what the papers had to say in the aftermath.

Town top-four win at Central Park

A match etched into the folklore of Cumbrian Rugby League was Workington's win over Wigan in the top-four play-off in 1951 as Town headed for their Championship Final glory against Warrington. This picture shows Town's Aussie centre Tony Paskins on the fly at Central Park as Wigan prop Ken Gee covers.

Our boys ready to win World Cup

Great Britain players at Headingley preparing for the 1972 World Cup. Left to right: David Jeanes, Brian Lockwood, Mick Stephenson, Terry Clawson, David Topliss, Steve Nash, Dennis O'Neill, Phil Lowe and David Redfearn.

The information in your pocket

As reassuring as the smell of linament and clattering of studs as each summer entered its final weeks and another new season got ready to kick off, Rugby League fans would get their information up to date with the unmissable books which appeared at the start of every new campaign. The Rugby Football League's *"Official Guide"* - the little blue book - was the game's essential handbook. Then came the *"Eddie Waring Annual,"* bright, brash, breezy, colourful ... just like Eddie himself and full of stories about the stars. Both books small enough to fit in your pocket but packed with info.

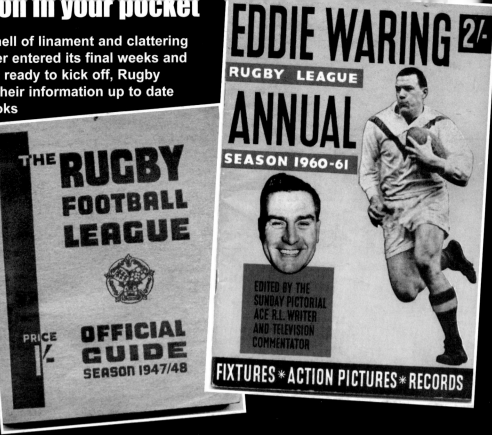

(Below) Station Road at Swinton saw many dramatic moments in staging Challenge Cup semi-finals, with one of the most famous tries being scored by Leeds flyer John Atkinson in 1968 against Wigan. Our photo captures Atkinson swerving his way through the Wigan defence as he wrong-foots full-back Colin Tyrer on the way to the great try which helped take Leeds to Wembley.

Cup semi-finals at Station Road

(Above) A taste of Anglo-French action as Duggie Greenall, on home turf at Knowsley Road, fires through the French defence whilst playing for a *"Rugby League X111"* in 1958. On the right is his Saints colleague Tom Van Vollenhoven on the wing. France beat a star-studded select team 26-8.

Stepping out in Bayonne

(Left) Alan Burwell of Hull Kingston Rovers leads out the Great Britain Under-24 team, alongside his French counterpart Herve Mazard, at Bayonne on 26th November, 1966. It was only the third match between the two Euro-nations at Under-24 level and France won 7-4. The stadium in Bayonne has, in recent years, been renamed in memory of Jean Dauger, one of the greats of French rugby in both codes.

(Right) Wales versus France in the European Championship in 1978, and Colin Dixon is the Welshman with the ball as Paul Woods is in support. The French player on the floor trying to make the tackle is scrum-half Jean-Marie Imbert from Avignon. Colin Dixon gave great service to both Halifax and Salford and was a Lions tourist in 1974.

The Referee on the spot

But did he give a try? This Hull Kingston Rovers man appears to have been grounded just inches short playing against Leeds at Headingley in the early 1960s. His Robins colleagues in close support are Alvin Ackerley and John Taylor, whilst for the Loiners Jack Fairbank makes a last ditch challenge as Welsh scrum-half Colin Evans looks on anxiously.

Sergeant Major at Oldham

The game's best known referee, Eric Clay, keeps a close watch on things in this match at the Watersheddings in September 1958, as Workington Town winger Ken Faulder tackles Oldham's Syd Little. On the right, is the tough Welsh forward Charlie Winslade.

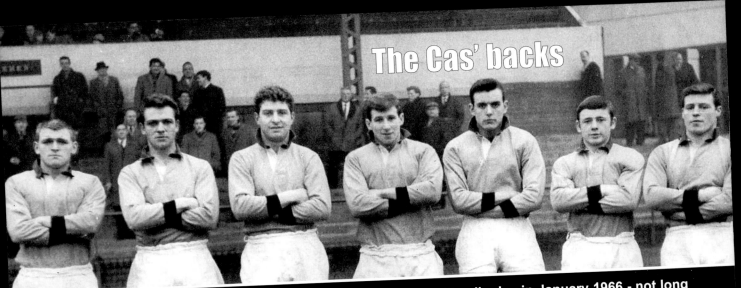

The Cas' backs

The Castleford back division line up before playing Leeds at Headingley in January 1966 - not long after Cas' decided that one of these bright young prospects was surplus to requirements so they transferred him to Hull K.R., where he managed to carve out a pretty fair career in the game. We won't ask you to guess which one that was! The line up is, *left to right:* Derek Edwards, Colin Battye, Malcolm Battye, Ron Willett, Trevor Briggs, Roger Millward and Keith Hepworth.

You can read all about it

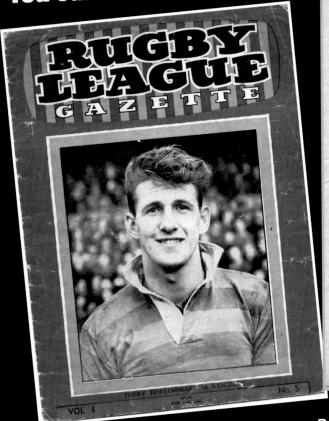

RUGBY LEAGUE GAZETTE

TERRY HOLLINDRAKE of KEIGHLEY

PRICE
ONE SHILLING

VOL 4   No. 5

RUGBY LEAGUE REVIEW

The Monthly Journal of Rugby League Football

No. 10 Vol. I   JUNE 1947   Price 7D.

IN THIS ISSUE:
FOOTBALLER
BROTHERS.
CUP FINAL SCENES
DEWSBURY
"SPOTLIGHT"

THE FAVOURITES FINALE!

By "THOR"

Our Special Representative's Impressions of the Cup Final

THE volume of sound which greeted the appearance of the Leeds team left no doubt as to who were favourites in this year's Wembley Final! Their record merited this distinction, but as usual their opponents were far from overawed. Bradford won because of superior tactics, while Leeds lost because of their lack of adaptability and inelasticity. I am convinced that the plan of campaign which had been so very successful against Wigan and Wakefield Trinity contributed

to the downfall of the side in the Final.

The success of their forward play led Leeds to believe that this type of game would be all that was required. When this failed to come off they had no alternative line of attack.

The men from Headingley, as so often in the past, were a team of brilliant individualists without any cohesive plan of combination.

(Continued overleaf)

Back Row: B. Tyler, H. Eva
Middle Row: J. Kitching, B. I
Front Row

RUGBY LEAGUE MAGAZINE

Vol. 3   No. 34

Price
One Shilling

KEITH JARRETT

Barrow's new
signing from
Wales

Photo courtesy 'Daily Mail'

The enthusiasm for producing magazines on Rugby League was always strong, despite the many difficulties involved. Three familiar examples here: *"Rugby League Gazette"* - this one from early 1957 and featuring Keighley's Terry Hollindrake on the cover - appeared in several different formats throughout the 1950s. *"Rugby League Review"* the ground-breaking journal of Huddersfield's Stanley Chadwick, produced from 1947 to the mid '50s. And the pocket-sized *"Rugby League Magazine"* edited and published by another respected Huddersfield man,

Ike touches down

(Above) A familiar sight for Workington Town fans as Ike Southward touches down in the corner in front of the grandstand at Derwent Park in a Cup tie against Rochdale in 1962, just outpacing the Hornets big Fijian winger Joe Levula. Ike passed away in 2006, but will never be forgotten.

(Below) With their shift at work finished, it was down the Lane to training on a frosty winter's night for these Castleford players pictured in February 1961. They are, from left to right: Brown (holding ball), Hepworth, Tonkinson, Sheridan (peeping through the pack), Bridges, Pye and Bryant. Behind in the striped jersey is Sayer. These lads wouldn't be off playing golf in the afternoons!

Training down Wheldon Lane

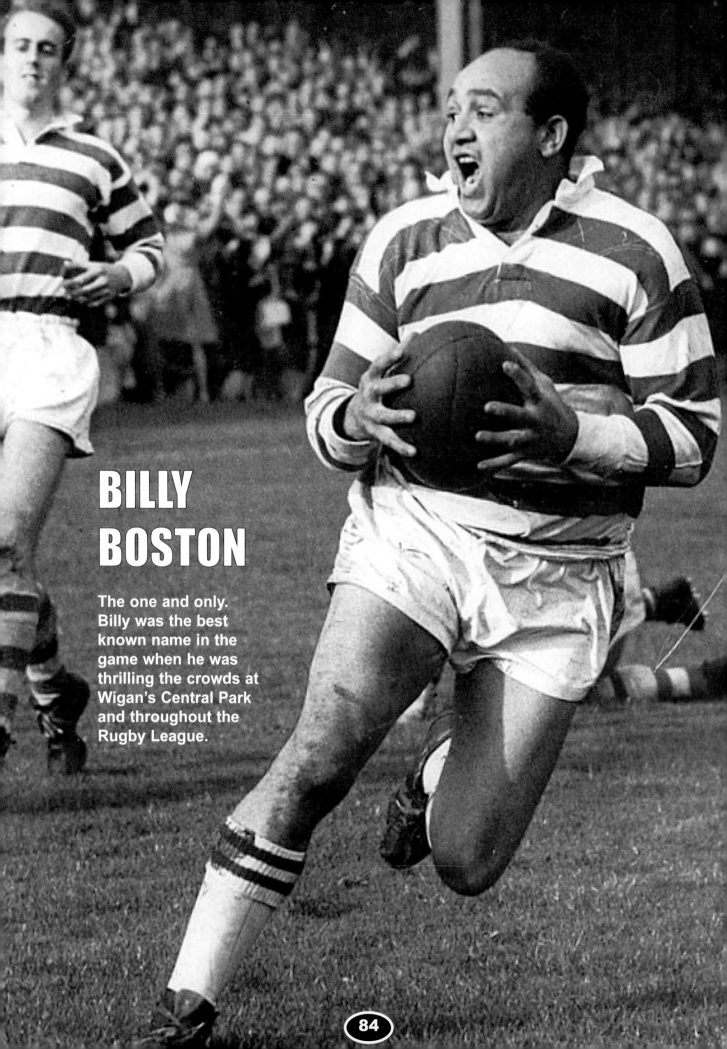

BILLY BOSTON

The one and only. Billy was the best known name in the game when he was thrilling the crowds at Wigan's Central Park and throughout the Rugby League.

THE LOINERS

(Above) The Leeds team of 1947 pictured before playing Wakefield Trinity at Fartown in the semi-final of the Challenge Cup. Leeds won 21-nil to go on to Wembley where they were narrowly beaten in the Cup Final by Bradford Northern, 8-4. They are, left to right: *(Standing):* "Dolly" Dawson (Coach), Bert Cook, Dai Prosser, Chris Brereton, Alec Watson, Arthur Clues, Con Murphy, Dai Jenkins. *(In front):* Tommy Cornelius, Gareth Price, Dickie Williams, Ike Owens, T.L.Williams, E.C.Whitehead.

(Right) KEVIN DICK in possession for Leeds in the 1979 Premiership Final against Bradford Northern played at Huddersfield's Fartown ground. Half-back Dick won the Harry Sunderland memorial trophy as man-of-the-match as Leeds beat their West Yorkshire rivals 24-2. The full Leeds team that day was: Neil Hague; Alan Smith, David Smith, Les Dyl, John Atkinson; Kevin Dick, John "Sammy" Sanderson; Mick Harrison, David Ward, Steve Pitchford, Graham Joyce, Graham Eccles and Phil Cookson.

BRIAN BEVAN
The game's greatest try-scorer

He didn't look like most folk's idea of a Rugby League player, but he was the greatest try-scorer the game has ever seen. Brian Bevan remains one of the true legends of the game - his incredible total of 788 tries in senior football never to be overtaken. Bevan spent 17 seasons with Warrington from 1945-46 to 1961-62, plus a further two with Blackpool Borough as he wound down his wonderful career. The picture above shows one of those tries, at Wilderspool against Swinton - and just look how the crowd are mesmerised by Bevan as he dives over.

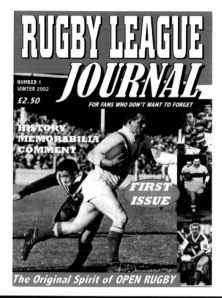
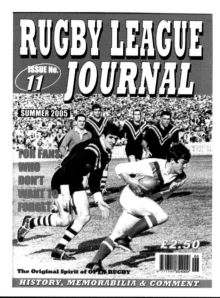
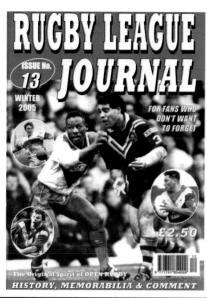
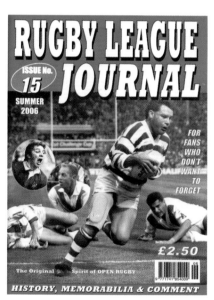

Australia v New Zealand

TESTMATCH

$6.00

STUART & McCLENNAN
COACHES WITH THE
MIDAS TOU

FRANK
PRITCHARD
From Sleeping
Giant To Tsunami

REMEMBER
1971?
Kiwis' Brief
Moment
In The Sun

HEROES OF
THE PAST
Olsen Filipaina
Bill Wilson

Andrew Johns
TRIBUTE TO A
CHAMPION

Bundaberg
LEAGUE
TEST
ARL

INSIDE: THE GREATEST TRANS-TASMAN CLASHES

SUNCORP STADIUM
is a non smoking venue
TICKETEK
2006 BUNDABERG RUM TEST
AUSTRALIA v NEW ZEALAND
SOUTHERN STAND
Fri 5 May 2006 7:30pm Gates 4:15pm
Free Public Transport - Conditions Apply

GATE	AISLE	ROW	SEAT	ADULT inc GST
A	509	42	48	$35.90

GATE
A
AISLE
509

The Queenslanders dominated

IT was a year of Queensland domination for Australian Rugby League in 2006, with the Maroons taking a pulsating State of Origin series followed by the Brisbane Broncos winning the Premiership - both the victorious teams being captained magnificently by Darren Lockyer.

The State of Origin series yet again lit up mid-winter in Australia as a new look Queensland side coached for the first time by their former centre and Kangaroo captain Mal Meninga, came back to overcome every kind of adversity to become deserved winners and so prevent an unprecedented fourth consecutive series loss.

With a host of young players making their Queensland debuts, the Maroons started the opening game in Sydney nervously before coming back to dominate. It took a last minute drop-goal by New South Wales scrum-half Brett Finch to edge the Blues home 19-18, but from that point onwards the series belonged to Lockyer and his Queensland team. A stunning 30-6 win in game two in Brisbane set up a decider staged on neutral territory in Melbourne in which the Maroons had to overcome some absolutely awful video referee decisions that, as the game went into its closing stages, looked as if they were going to rob Queensland of the victory they clearly deserved.

Mal Meninga, the victorious Queensland coach, happy after the deciding match.

That's where fate stepped in and, from 14-4 down with only nine minutes left on the clock, Lockyer inspired the comeback that led to a 16-14 win and him being the winning captain who stepped up to receive the Origin shield from the Queensland legend (and Lockyer's own boyhood hero) Wally Lewis.

Better was to follow for Lockyer as he led the Brisbane Broncos to a Premiership title that had looked so unlikely earlier in the season as they endured a long losing streak, and even after the first round of the play-offs when they were hammered at home by St.George-Illawarra. Brisbane won the Grand Final 15-8 over Melbourne Storm to claim the club's sixth Premiership since they entered the competition in 1988. In doing so they overcame a Melbourne team which had been the N.R.L.'s best team all year, finishing top of the table eight points clear of the team in second place (Canterbury.) Brisbane finished third fully 12 points behind Melbourne. In that Grand Final it was Melbourne who were on the receiving end of some wrong refereeing decisions, which was very harsh luck on their brilliant young talents like Billy Slater, Greg Inglis and the new whizz-kid scrum half Cooper Cronk.

The Grand Final made history as the first not to include a team from Sydney. Fears that having two out of state clubs contest the big game would lower the crowd proved to be unfounded as the usual capacity 82,000 attendance packed the Olympic Stadium in Sydney. But even the most one-eyed Sydneysiders would have to concede that Queensland held the ascendency in 2006 with not just the Broncos in the Grand Final but also the fact that the Melbourne team had such a strong Queensland foundation to it, based on their long-held link up with the Queensland Cup teams as feeder-clubs. In total, there were 17 Queensland State of Origin players on he field in the Grand Final.

Melbourne's coach Craig Bellamy (a Queenslander and prodigy and former assistant of Wayne Bennett) was a virtually unanimous choice as the NRL's Coach-of-the-year, whilst the Melbourne captain Cameron Smith (the Queensland hooker) was the prestigious *"Dally M."* winner as the Australian game's Player-of-the-year.

That Queensland strength and the continued production line of highly talented young players augers well for the arrival of the new club in the NRL next year, the Gold Coast Titans.

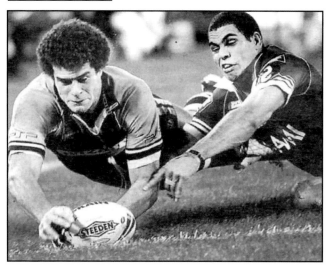

(Above) **Matt King dives over to score for NSW in the first State of Origin match of 2006, just beating Queensland's Greg Inglis. Both King and Inglis starred in the Melbourne team which finished top of the NRL in Australia.**

Overall the game continued to be in rude good health in Australia in terms of public support and with a massive new television deal about to be signed. Average attendances for the regular season club match attendances were slightly down on last year's record figures, but much of this was an inevitable result of the traditionally big crowd-pullers in Sydney: Easts (that's the Roosters to those who

Pictured on opposite page: Australia said goodbye to Andrew Johns in the Anzac Test of 2006 and Queensland won the State of Origin. Action as Willie Mason scores for NSW, then Darren Lockyer dives over for the series winner in Melbourne. In the Anzac Test the Aussie team salutes Johns and full-back Karmichael Hunt made his international debut against New Zealand.

know no better), Parramatta and St.George, spending much of the year in the lower reaches of the table. Easts, for so long the richest glamour club in Sydney, dropped dramatically to next to bottom on the table and finished up sacking their coach Ricky Stuart (in his first year as the Australian national team coach) and parting company with several high profile players - among them Englishman Adrian Morley.

Parramatta also changed their coach mid-season after an unsuccessful start, the influential Brian Smith stepping down to be replaced by former scrum-half Jason Taylor who sparked a revival which saw the Eels rise to claim a play-off spot. St.George, likewise, came good in the end and got through to the last hurdle before the Grand Final.

Brian Smith - once of Hull and Bradford - left the coaching job at Parramatta mid-season.

The biggest attendances were obtained by the Brisbane Broncos - playing at the refurbished Suncorp Stadium (Lang Park) - they touched 50,000 on occasions taking the Broncos back to the heights of the pre-Super League days. That appetite for the game in Brisbane was reinforced by a crowd of 44,141 attending the Anzac Test between Australia and New Zealand on 5th May 2006. That was the biggest for a Test against the Kiwis for over 40 years.

Part of the attraction was the chance to see the Aussies take their revenge on the Kiwis for the shock defeat in the final of the 2005 Tri Nations in England, and also to say farewell to the brilliant Andrew Johns playing his last game in the green and gold. On both counts the Brisbane crowd were not disappointed as the Australian team, with Lockyer and Johns the half-backs and the brilliant Timana Tahu back on the wing, were unrecognisable to the team which had been embarrassed 24-nil in Leeds by New Zealand. Likewise, the Kiwis without Stacey Jones, were rudderless at half-back and despite a fierce physical effort by their forwards, could not live with the sheer class of Johns, Lockyer and company.

Steve Menzies - the Manly forward back in the Australian team in 2006.

Loose-forward Ben Kennedy was another, like Johns, playing his last international for Australia, but there were no such thoughts from the Manly second-rower Steve Menzies, back in the Australian team he first played for way back in 1994. And the best farewell of the the year down-under came when Shane Webcke bowed out with a Grand Final win for Brisbane - the mighty prop has stood for all that is best about Rugby League and it was fitting that he brought the curtain down on such a fine career in such successful style.

The Australian team which beat New Zealand 50-12 in the 2006 Anzac Test was: Karmichael Hunt (Brisbane); Matt King (Melbourne), Mark Gasnier (St.George), Matt Cooper (St.George), Timana Tahu (Parramatta); Darren Lockyer (Brisbane) Captain, Andrew Johns (Newcastle); Willie Mason (Canterbury-Bankstown), Danny Buderus (Newcastle), Petero Civaniceva (Brisbane), Luke O'Donnell (North Queensland), Nathan Hindmarsh (Parramatta), Ben Kennedy (Manly-Warringah). *Substitutes:* Jonathan Thurston (North Queensland), Mark O'Meley (Canterbury-Bankstown), Steve Menzies (Manly-Warringah) and Steve Simpson (Newcastle). The coach was Ricky Stuart.

Aussies honour their 'greats'

AUSTRALIAN Rugby League loves to honour its traditions and its great players of the past, and that continued in 2006 with the election of more men to their "Hall of Fame" and the creation of their Australian *"Team of the Sixties."* Truly that decade was a golden era for the international game and some of the Kangaroos' finest moments came in the 1960s - so it was no surprise that some of the game's best loved characters were included, with the mighty St.George club dominating the selection with six representatives.

The Australian *"Team of the Sixties"* was: **Les Johns** (Canterbury-Bankstown); **Ken Irvine** (North Sydney), **Reg Gasnier** (St.George), **Graeme Langlands** (St.George), **Johnny King** (St.George); **Bob Fulton** (Manly-Warringah), **Billy Smith** (St.George); **Arthur Beetson** (Balmain), **Ian Walsh** (St.George), **Noel Kelly** (Wests), **Dick Thornett** (Parramatta), **Ron Coote** (Souths) and **Johnny Raper** (St.George).

(Pictured right) Arthur Beetson playing for Australia against France in the 1972 World Cup. The French player on the right is Carlos Zalduendo, better known in recent years as the President of the Toulouse Olympique club.

RUGBY League in New Zealand began 2006 with a real spring in its step following the Kiwis' victory in the Tri-Nations tournament at the end of the previous year. The Kiwis' reward was to be able to stage their games against Great Britain at home on New Zealand soil in the 2006 Tri-Nations.

The N.Z. Rugby League also reported a record profit on last year - figures which were miniscule in comparison to those we know in the British and Australian game, but significant for the New Zealanders where Rugby League struggles to generate major commercial support in the media shadow of the all-embracing All Blacks. That profit came as a direct result of the success of the Kiwis' international matches played in Australia and England where much bigger attendances can be attracted than in New Zealand. This, allied to the weakness of the N.Z. dollar on the currency exchanges, means it is much, much more profitable for the Kiwis to play overseas than at home. The result is that the annual Anzac Test is now set to be played in Australia permanently, and there will be a few nervous moments before this year's Tri-Nations fixtures with Great Britain are staged in Wellington and Christchurch, after playing the Aussies in Auckland.

(Above) **Lusi Sione pictured with the New Zealand Residents team in 2006. The former Workington Town full-back returned home during the year and quickly re-established himself with the Canterbury Bulls team.**

On the field, the immediate aftermath to the 2005 Tri-Nations glory wasn't that great for coach Brian McClennan and his Kiwi team. Flogged 50 points to 12 by Australia in Brisbane in the Anzac Test (although the treasurer would be happy again with a huge crowd of over 44,000 at the game), and then seeing his New Zealand X111 (it wasn't the full Kiwi side as so many top players were unavailable) heavily beaten by Great Britain in a mid-season encounter at St.Helens, left more questions than answers.

New Zealand now has a huge number of Australian-based players available to them, alongside those emerging through the New Zealand Warriors professonal club in Auckland - many of them big, powerful and aggressive athletes - but it desperately needs to find some creative and skilful half-backs to try and fill the shoes of Stacey Jones. It also needs to find a way to ensure its best young stars like Benji Marshall, Matt Utai and Sonny-Bill Williams can stop being injured every time the Tri-Nations comes around.

On the club front the Warriors, on whom so much of the game's health in New Zealand is now based, had a solid rather than spectacularly successful season in the N.R.L. Under their new coach, Australian Ivan Cleary, and with experienced props Ruben Wiki and Steven Price

laying the foundation, the Warriors finished in tenth position, just two away from making the play-offs. Had they not been docked four points for a salary cap breach in 2005, the Warriors would have overtaken Parramatta and qualified for the play-offs.

Domestically, New Zealand's Bartercard Card Cup cometition got a boost by with a new deal with Maori Television to broadcast games live on Monday nights. The Cup - effectively New Zealand's National club competition - was won by the Auckland Lions who beat the Canterbury Bulls 27-14 in the Final. It was the third season in a row that these two teams had contested the Final with the same winners each time. Coached by Kiwi boss Brian McClennan and captained by Steve Buckingham, the Auckland Lions were effectively the Mount Albert club team playing under a manufactured guise. And many people in New Zealand recognise that the Bartercard Cup games struggle to attract crowds, whereas the local club competitions do much better, because supporters have genuine club loyalties and there is local community support for the traditional clubs rather than manufactured "franchises."

Stars for the Canterbury Bulls team included the two recently returned former Workington Town favourites, Jonny Limmer and Lusi Sione. Both also played for the New Zealand Residents team.

Mount Albert also won the Auckland competition, for the Fox Memorial Shield, hammering Papakura 49-6 in the Final played at Mount Smart Stadium. In Christchurch, Hornby emerged as the champion club as they beat Linwood 32-28 in their Final; whilst in the capital city of Wellington, Petone overcame the defending champions North City 26-18 to win their Final and take the Appleton Shield.

In a nice touch of recognition of the game's roots in New Zealand, the full Kiwi Test team was scheduled to play a match at Wingham Park, Greymouth on the West Coast for the first time in 52 years. During their week off in the Tri-Nations, the Kiwis will play the New Zealand Residents team, at the same ground where N.Z. played Great Britain in a Test match back in 1954. At that time, Greymouth was regarded as the smallest town anywhere in the world to stage a Test match, played in homage to the West Coast, one of the great traditional strongholds of the game on the south island of New Zealand, where coalmining and Rugby League went hand in hand.

ALL eyes in French Rugby League in the year 2006 were focussed on Perpignan and the debut of the Catalans team in Super League. Of course, there were plenty of valid arguments over the wisdom of having so much emphasis being placed on a single club playing in an English competition - just as there were growing concerns this year of the rather dubious benefits of having French clubs travel to Britain to play in the Challenge Cup - but once the "Dragons" had arrived in Super League, all doubts had to be forgotten and all hands turned to positive efforts to ensure the project was a success.

The French Rugby League community rallied admirably around the Catalans. It was recognsised that, in the absence of any other financial investment in the domestic game, having the full-time "Dragons" club in Super League was the only way to present *Rugby a XIII* to the French media and public as a serious, professional sport rather than the small-time, almost "village," game it was in danger of becoming.

"It is the antibiotic our ailing game desperately needed," said Jacques Jorda, the charismatic former coach of the French national team (still best remembered for being at the helm when France beat Great Britain at Headingley in 1990.) Meanwhile, the current President of the French Rugby League, Nicolas Larrat, described the Catalans' Super League adventure as *"Our shop window."*

On that score, the "Dragons" didn't let anybody down. They may have been very disappointed to finish bottom of the table, but in doing so they achieved 16 points from eight wins and proved themselves, certainly at home, to be very competitive. The guidance of overseas imports like skipper Stacey Jones - and, during his absence, young Michael Dobson - may have been crucial, but it was pleasing the way numerous young French players, in their first season at this level, proved themselves to be competitive against the full-time pros' of Super League. That can only auger well for the French national team in the future, which was the other important *raison d'etre* for having a French club in Super League.

So, what kind of impact did the Catalans "Dragons" have for Rugby League in their own country? The

Julien Rinaldi, the French national team captain, had a good season with the Catalans.

Maxime Greseque makes the break that led to Pia's winning try in the closing minutes of the 2006 French Championship Final against Toulouse, and thus clinched the "double."

wider French sports media still largely refused to give them any kind of recognition or positive coverage, but within the *Treiziste* community itself the impact was very positive, especially after a deal was done to finance television coverage of the Catalans' games on the cable channel *Sport +*. After a fine opening occasion against Wigan drew an 11,000 plus crowd, the "Dragons" announced their average home attendance for the season as 6,542. Considering the existing low level of crowds for club games in France, this was a very encouraging figure, especially as the club had to play four of their home games away from Perpignan due the *Stade Aime Giral* beng unavailable to them. The match against Castleford, which brought the Catalans' biggest win of the campaign, was taken to Carcassonne and, predictably, drew an excellent crowd in an area that still remains the hotbed of Rugby League interest despite the problems of the local club.

Within the city of Perpignan itself, the Catalans in Super League was a very popular success with the local business community as they welcomed an influx of thousands of English supporters every few weeks throughout the season.

So, as a promotional vehicle for the game in France and a player-development exercise, the Catalans "Dragons" project was launched with no little success. Next year the huge challenge is to improve on that - and they will try to do it playing back at the old home of Rugby League in Perpignan, a refurbished *Stade Gilbert Brutus,* and without a significant number of the established French players who did them proud in their debut season but have now either retired, or not been retained.

Those who are retiring include forward Pascal Jampy and stand-off Laurent Frayssinous. Both have given long and dedicated service to the French team through some desperately difficult years - Jampy making his Test debut back in 1993 against the Kiwis, and Frayssinous as part of the international half-back partnership with Julien Rinaldi which was a key part of the Villeneuve team which helped pioneer new standards of professionalism in the French game. As for Rinaldi, he enjoyed a very good debut season in Super League, being employed by his Aussie coaches in the hooker/dummy-half role rather than his more familiar scrum-half position. But he, too, is finished with the Catalans and is moving to London to play for Harlequins in 2007.

In his role as captain of the French national team, Rinaldi had led them in the latter months of 2005 to victory in the Euro Nations Cup by beating Wales 38-16 in Carcassonne; followed by defeats in two Tests - 44-12

A picture for the history books - the Catalans Dragons in their debut season in the Super League, including Australian mentor David Waite, coach Mick Potter, guest player Mick Dobson and captain Stacey Jones with his broken arm in plaster. Many of these players won't be involved in the second year, but they were the ones who launched the project.

against Australia in Perpignan and 38-22 against New Zealand in Toulouse. In these games France were coached by the Australian John Monie, once of Wigan.

Domestically, 2006 was a tough year for the game in France as it got down to life without its own leading club in Perpignan - crowds continued to dwindle in the Championship, but the widely predicted dominance of Toulouse Olympique once the Catalans had being taken out of the equation did not materialise. Instead it was the village club of Pia who outshone all their rivals to claim both the Championship and the Lord Derby Cup - the first time in their history that they had won the "double."

The Cup win came 31 years since Pia's only previous triumph in the competition, and was completed by a 36-20 victory in the Final over Lezignan. Played at Carcassonne at its traditional time of mid-May, the Lord Derby Cup Final drew an official attendance of 9,344.

Better was to come for Pia in the Championship Final against Toulouse Olympique. Played in Toulouse at the home stadium of the city's Rugby Union club, Pia won 21-18, but it took them until the 75th minute of the match to get their noses in front for the first time. Pia's winning try by Australian second-rower Neil Wyatt coming after a thrilling run by their captain and inspiration, Maxime Greseque. It put the seal on a great achievement for Pia but, played on the first weekend of July in what was described as a "furnace" with temperatures in excess of 37 degrees, it also proved the final deathknell for the folly of trying to play summer rugby in France.

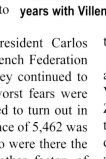

VINCENT WULF - ten years with Villeneuve.

The influential Toulouse club president Carlos Zalduendo had already threatened the French Federation that he would pull out of the game if they continued to mess around with the season, and the worst fears were confirmed when *Treiziste* supporters failed to turn out in numbers for the Final. An official attendance of 5,462 was issued by the Federation, but to those who were there the crowd looked considerably smaller. Another factor, of course, was Pia's inability to mobilise support in large numbers compared to some of the bigger towns.

For those who try to compare standards, it did not reflect well on the French game when Pia, the team who were dominating their domestic competitions and went on to win the "double," were outclassed 70 points to nil by Whitehaven in the Challenge Cup. There were mitigating circumstances for Pia, who travelled to England without several of their senior players, including their talisman Maxime Greseque - but it didn't look good.

The fact that a tiny village like Pia - boosted by at least half a dozen Antipodean imports in their team each time they took the field - came out on top in French Rugby League, was a reflection of the size of the problems the game faces in France. Both Limoux and St.Gaudens continued to be the strongest challengers to Pia and Toulouse, and Lezignan - a club that almost went bust the previous year - got a huge boost by winning through to the Lord Derby Cup Final. But there was no sign yet of a revival by Carcassonne - always regarded as the "sleeping giant" of French Rugby League.

The weakness of the Championship was illustrated when Marseille dropped out early in the season after it became apparent they had no money, and despite clubs like Carpentras and Lyon-Villeurbanne being uncompetitive in the Elite Division, no club was strong enough to put itself forward for promotion from the lower division - including the once mighty Racing Club of Albi, who found their presence dwindle even further as the Albi Rugby Union club won promotion to the high profile "Top 14" and began to dominate their local sporting scene in a town where Rugby League was always regarded previously as the number one.

Among the players retiring in 2006 was Vincent Wulf, a man who has given over a decade of fine service to both Villeneuve and the French game after arriving from New Zealand in 1995. Vince played for Paris St.Germain in their debut season in 1996 and, after qualifying on residential grounds, was the regular hooker for France for several years, including in the 2000 World Cup. He was given a "Jubilee" (Testimonial) by Villeneuve in 2006 and is taking up a coaching role in the new season.

THE 2005-06 season saw teams from the east of the Pennines dominate the top level of Amateur Rugby League. Not only did Yorkshire win the County Championship, but clubs from the land of the white rose also won both the Amateur game's top competitions - the BARLA National Cup and the Premier Division of the National Conference.

Skirlaugh, the village club from near Hull, set a new record when they stormed to their fourth National Cup success, beating Leigh Miners 26-13 in another uplifting Final played at Blackpool's Bloomfield Road. Captained by that great servant at prop Phil Crane, who was making a record fifth Final appearance, Skirlaugh lived up to their favourites tag, making it a joyous occasion for their coach Richard Gotts who, himself, had captained them to previous National Cups in 1996 and 2000. Skirlaugh centre Matt Danville was voted man-of-the-match, and was awarded the famous sword trophy in memory of the founding secretary of BARLA, the late Tom Keaveney.

On their way to the Final at Blackpool, Skirlaugh had narrowly negotiated the hurdle of their old rivals Wath Brow, knocking the gallant Hornets out of both the BARLA Cup and the Rugby League Challenge Cup as the Cumbrians made the coast-to-coast journey to Humberside twice in successive weeks. Once they had got Wath Brow out of the way, Skirlaugh sensed it was going to be their year, but not before they had overcome a strong Leigh Miners team who had ended a 23-year wait to appear in their fourth National Cup Final after being the inaugral winners of the trophy way back in 1973.

In the league competition, Oulton became National Conference Champions by beating Thornhill 20-11 in the play-off Grand Final at Mount Pleasant, Batley. At the end of a long, hard season full of excellent football in the Conference, the Grand Final was an emotion-charged and action-packed occasion which ended in drama and shame as yobs in the crowd caused violent scenes when the trophy was being presented to Oulton. Those yobs brought disgrace on the Thornhill club who were subsequently penalised by having four points deducted from their 2006-07 league campaign.

None of that should distract from Oulton's achievement, and most people would say their Grand Final win was deserved as they had finished the season as leaders of the Conference Premier Division by a point from Wigan St.Patrick's, with Thornhill in fourth spot behind Leigh Miners. In the Conference Division One, the promotion places were won by West Hull and West Bowling, and in Division Two by Castleford Panthers and Widnes St.Maries.

For the club from the Heavy Woollen district, Thornhill, the events at the end of the Grand Final took the shine off what had been a tremendous season for them. They illustrated, yet again, the strength of the top BARLA

The Rugby League's official magazine - formerly known as the *"BARLA Bulletin"* - features Skirlaugh captain Phil Crane proudly lifting the Amateurs' National Cup after their victory over Leigh Miners in the final at Blackpool in 2006.

clubs by knocking a professional club out of the Challenge Cup - Workington Town being their unfortunate victims - which set up a trip to France to play the new Super League side, the Catalans Dragons. And in captain Anthony Broadhead they had the outstanding player in the Amateur game, the back-rower being named as BARLA's Open-Age player-of-the-year.

But when it came to representative football, Broadhead found himself one of the players caught up in the politcal wrangling that continued to bedevil Amateur Rugby League in the aftermath of the supposed "reunification" between BARLA and the RFL. With the Great Britain Amateur team now under the jurisdiction of the game's "Community Board," it was hard to believe that a fixture was arranged for the BARLA rep. team (which still was referred to in the media as "BARLA Great Britain") in the Public Servants Cup competition, on the very same night that the G.B. Amateurs were playing their home international against France. Anthony Broadhead captained the Yorkshire-dominated BARLA team.

Meanwhile, the Great Britain Amateurs were being beaten 11-10 by a very enthusiastic French side at Batley in an entertaining match worthy of a far bigger audience than the handful of spectators who turned up. The game's top amateur players, who put in so much time and commitment, deserve far, far better. After recording a close 26-22 win in France back in November against a very young French *"Espoirs"* side, the Great Britain side found themselves up against a little more Open-Age opposition in the return match at Batley. Inspired by Limoux scrum-half Mickael Murcia, *"France B"* deserved their 11-10 victory at a rain-swept Mount Pleasant. The Great Britain side was again captained by prop Paul Davidson of Wath Brow Hornets.

The high quality of players continuing to be produced by the BARLA clubs was again illustrated by the fact that, within weeks of playing in the Amateur international, both David Whitworth and Scott Teare were standing out in first team football in the professional ranks, for Workington and Whitehaven respectively. Perhaps the time-held production line is best recognised in Cumbria, where last season's BARLA Youth Great Britain Under-18 captain Scott McAvoy also made the immediate leap from Hensingham to first-grade with Whitehaven and was outstanding against all the top sides in National League One. It was that success in producing top class players for the professional game that saw the remarkable rise of Wath Brow Hornets suffer a break in momentum, after an incredible three years which had seen them join the National Conference and go up through the divisions as Champions each year, win back-to-back National Cups and provide such romantic exploits against professional clubs in the Challenge Cup.

It was, perhaps, inevitable that the West Cumbrians would become victims of their own success, with no less than six of their trophy-winning team moving on to play for Whitehaven - Craig Calvert, Derry Eilbeck, Carl Rudd, Mark Deans, Graeme Mattinson and Scott Teare.

Elsewhere, BARLA representative teams enjoyed a mini-tour to Italy in the summer, taking a mix of Open-Age and Youth players, and also rose above all opposition to win the Middlesex International Nines tournament

Flashback to 2003 and four Cumbrians in the BARLA Great Britain team pictured before they achieved a remarkable victory over the full French international team - Carl Rudd, Eddie Robinson, Scott Teare and Paul Davidson. Of the Wath Brow trio, in 2006 both Rudd and Teare starred for Whitehaven in the professional ranks whilst Davidson continued to captain the Great Britain Amateurs. Robinson, meanwhile, helped take Ellenborough to the semi-final of the National Cup.

played in London on the weekend of the Challenge Cup Final. And Amateur players have much to look forward to at international level in the near future, with plans to re-launch the traditional BARLA versus Australian Aboriginals series plus a possible tour to South Africa.

At Youth level, BARLA's player-of-the-year was Lewis Lilley from West Hull, whilst the launch of the new National Youth League was deemed a big success. Widnes St.Maries emerged as the first winners, beating Siddal 20-18 in a nail-biting Final played at the Shay, Halifax.

In the "Champion of Champions" end-of-season tournament featuring the winners of the BARLA major regional leagues, Halton Simms Cross retained the trophy, beating the Leeds side Queens, 27-nil, in a robust Final at Blackpool. Meanwhile, in the Women's Rugby League Challenge Cup Final, the mighty Wakefield Panthers once again took the the trophy, this year defeating Bradford Thunderbirds 43-4 in the Final played at Featherstone.

The Great Britain Amateurs team which played France at Batley in April 2006 was:

Mat Rogers (Eastmoor); **David Whitworth** (Ellenborough), **Martin Johnson** (East Hull), **Gavin Corfield** (Wigan St.Jude's), **Lee Heggarty** (Royal Marines/Navy); **Martin Ridyard** (Leigh Miners), **Danny Kilshaw** (Leigh East); **Scott Teare** (Wath Brow), **Liam Walsh** (Siddal), **Paul Davidson** (Wath Brow) Captain, **David Patterson** (Leigh Miners), **Simon Warhurst** (Leigh Miners), **Melvin Alker** (Wigan St.Patrick's). *Substitutes:* **John Cole** (Warrington Wizards), **David Hull** (Thatto Heath), **Adam Endersby** (York Acorn), **Andrew Rasburn** (Wigan St.Patrick's) and **Kevin Brown** (Eastmoor).

(Above) Memories of the BARLA Young Lions of almost 20 years ago, in action against the Junior Kiwis of New Zealand at Central Park, Wigan in 1987. Trevor Croston of Wigan St.Patrick's is the British player in possession - in support on the left (wearing the headguard) is hooker Jason Ramshaw, well known at Keighley.

New Horizons in 2006

THERE were very mixed fortunes for Rugby League in 2006 as it sought to continue breaking down its boundaries to reach new horizons. The good news was that in Wales, Scotland and Ireland, local summer leagues continued to expand and provide plenty of enjoyment, whilst further afield in Europe more new nations found themselves on the Rugby League map as several incredibly motivated enthusiasts progressed groups of park footballers to form national teams. The most solid of all the European developments appeared to be in Serbia, who were able to host English teams and send a team to France to play in a Euro-Under-19s tournament. A fascinating development, as Rugby League was previously played in Serbia (as part of the former Yugoslavia) back in the 1950s and early '60s.

The British Student Rugby League movement proved to be the key to helping the development of the game overseas, as they provided all four teams from the home nations to take part in that Under-19 tournament which was won convincingly by the host nation, France. And the British Students were also able to send a "Pioneers" team on a ground-breaking trip to the Czech Republic.

Meanwhile, at the top level of the Student game, the Great Britain team registered a 22-8 win over their old rivals France, before heading down-under for a three Test "Academic Ashes" tour to Australia. Unfortunately for the Brits, all three Tests were lost to the Aussies, 24-16 in both the first two games, and 34-14 in the third.

Both the ancient universities of Oxford and Cambridge continued to develop their scholarship programmes, but it was the very progressive Cambridge club who continued their dominance of the Varsity match. The light blues also got into the international mood, exchanging visits with the students of Nanterre (Paris) before flying off to the east coast of America for a successful off-season summer tour.

The continued expansion in playing numbers and improving standards of the Student game, which continues to play in the "traditional" autumn/winter season alongside the other football codes, contrasted with the problems encountered in 2006 by those who propogate a summer-only season for Rugby League. Whilst the summer Conference competitons continued to be enjoyed in new areas for the game all over the country, the Rugby Football League-sponsored National League Three found itself down to only nine teams, and this included two new entrants from Yorkshire amateur clubs - Featherstone Lions and Dewsbury Celtic - who had been unable to maintain BARLA National Conference standards and had dropped out. That hardly gave the impression of being the development flagship National League Three had hoped to be. Only three teams remained from outside the so-called "heartland" areas - Hemel Hemsptead and St.Albans in the south, and Gateshead Storm in the north east. And for the best established of this trio, Hemel Hempstead, a vibrant

Flashback ...the Hemel Hempstead trailblazers of 1983, pictured in Venice, Italy where they travelled with Yorkshire amateurs Oulton, to help promote the game by playing sevens. Hemel's founder Bob Brown is third from the left on the front row with the ball at his feet. The referee standing on the far right is Joe Chamberlain, the ex-Rochdale full-back.

league competition - as they had hoped National League Three would be - is a must. Hemel were celebrating their 25th anniversary in 2006, and they did so by qualifying for the Grand Final only for the expansionists' dreams to be shattered by Bramley. The well-drilled Yorkshire side, coached by ex-Leeds player Paul Cook and playing out of the excellent facilities of BARLA club Stanningley, won the National League Three title by beating Hemel 30-8.

Hemel have been the major success story of Rugby League development in England over the past quarter century, thanks to the efforts and guidance of their founder Bob Brown. Bob, who arrived in the U.K. from Australia in 1980, has proved how to put down real foundations for the sport in new areas and his views on the current policies of the RFL and some of their development activities in the south of England would make very uncomfortable reading for the powers-that-be.

In the Rugby League Conference, South London emerged as the champion team, winning the Harry Jepson trophy when they beat East Lancashire Lions 30-nil in the Premier League Grand Final staged at Coventry. In the Regional play-off, Liverpool Buccaneers were 36-30 winners over the Yorkshire side Thorne Moor Marauders.

The Powergen Champion Schools competitions continued to involve thousands of youngsters throughout the country, but the winners came from more familiar Rugby League territory - four of the six winning teams on Cup Final weekend coming from Yorkshire: Malet Lambert (Hull), Castleford High boys and Castleford High girls, and Holy Family (Keighley); plus Wade Deacon (Widnes) and St.John Fisher (Wigan). In total it was claimed that 25,000 pupils had participated in the competitions.

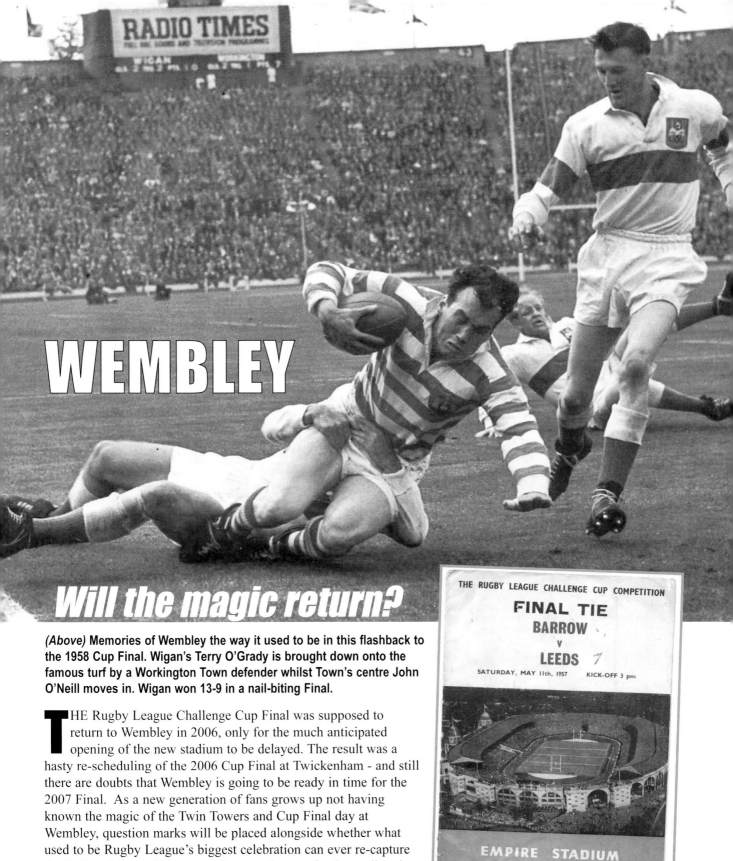

WEMBLEY

Will the magic return?

(Above) Memories of Wembley the way it used to be in this flashback to the 1958 Cup Final. Wigan's Terry O'Grady is brought down onto the famous turf by a Workington Town defender whilst Town's centre John O'Neill moves in. Wigan won 13-9 in a nail-biting Final.

THE RUGBY LEAGUE CHALLENGE CUP COMPETITION

FINAL TIE
BARROW
v
LEEDS

SATURDAY, MAY 11th, 1957   KICK-OFF 3 pm

EMPIRE STADIUM
WEMBLEY

OFFICIAL PROGRAMME · ONE SHILLING

THE Rugby League Challenge Cup Final was supposed to return to Wembley in 2006, only for the much anticipated opening of the new stadium to be delayed. The result was a hasty re-scheduling of the 2006 Cup Final at Twickenham - and still there are doubts that Wembley is going to be ready in time for the 2007 Final. As a new generation of fans grows up not having known the magic of the Twin Towers and Cup Final day at Wembley, question marks will be placed alongside whether what used to be Rugby League's biggest celebration can ever re-capture the feeling. Many of those new fans say they prefer the stadium in Cardiff, and the huge attraction of Old Trafford (truly now filling that old cliche about being "The Wembley of the north") has made the Super League Grand Final into a massive draw for all those clubs and groups who used to fill the old Wembley every year. Put that alongside the way the Challenge Cup has been devalued, and the longer the new Wembley is delayed, the more difficult it is going to be to recapture the magic.

The familiar Wembley programmes which were so sought after by the fans - this one for the 1957 Cup Final between Barrow and Leeds.

CARTOONISTS used to be a feature of most newspapers with the story of sporting events recorded by the skills of an art-form which appealed to fans both young and old. Rugby League was particularly well served by talented cartoonists who, throughout the gme's history, would caricature its heroes, villains and famous moments.

Among the best known names of cartoonists who told Rugby League's story were such as: "Nix," "Ern Shaw," "Edge," Frank Barton and Ken Adams - the latter who worked as big Jim Windsor's publicity manager for his pools business and was editor and illustrator of his famous "Windsors Rugby League Annual." It was a tradition which the old "Open Rugby" magazine tried to revive with much success thanks to the talent of cartoonists like Kevin Macey (creator of the character Arthur 'Ardbottom) and Dave Iddon (creator of Stan the Fan.)

The strip cartoon reproduced on this page was typical of its time by one of the best, "Edge" - this one was created in October 1960 to reflect on the World Cup decider in which Great Britain beat Australia 10-3 at a very wet Odsal Stadium. It was a game marred by violence and confrontations - perfect for a cartoonist to poke fun at!

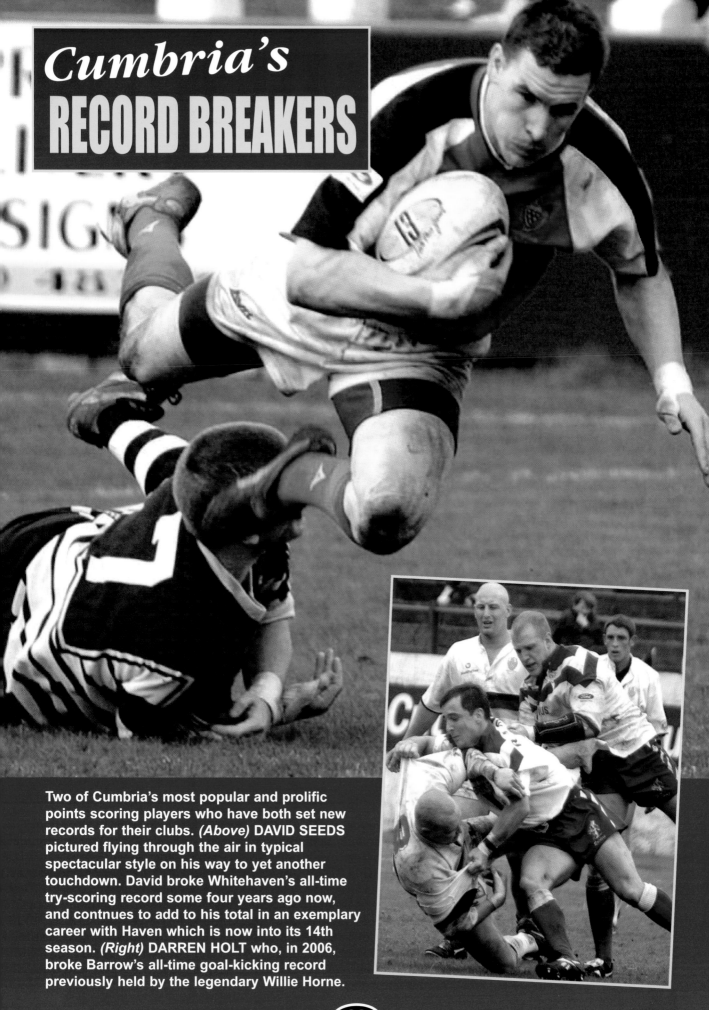

Cumbria's RECORD BREAKERS

Two of Cumbria's most popular and prolific points scoring players who have both set new records for their clubs. *(Above)* DAVID SEEDS pictured flying through the air in typical spectacular style on his way to yet another touchdown. David broke Whitehaven's all-time try-scoring record some four years ago now, and contnues to add to his total in an exemplary career with Haven which is now into its 14th season. *(Right)* DARREN HOLT who, in 2006, broke Barrow's all-time goal-kicking record previously held by the legendary Willie Horne.

RUGBY LEAGUE at CHELSEA

What would Mourinho say?

Rugby League International Match

BRITISH EMPIRE XIII
v.
NEW ZEALAND

Wednesday, 23rd January, 1952

STAMFORD BRIDGE GROUNDS LONDON S W 6
THE RIGHT OF ADMISSION TO GROUNDS IS RESERVED

OFFICIAL PROGRAMME

6d

Rugby League at Stamford Bridge - what would Chelsea's colourful manager Jose Mourinho *(pictured)* think of that?

There's little chance of it happening now, but in the past the 13-aside game has staged events at the stadium more widely known as the home of Chelsea football legends like Peter Osgood, "Chopper" Harris and company. In January, 1952, a British Empire X111 played the New Zealand touring team *(see the programme illustrated, left)* in a match staged on a Wednesday and which was notable as one of the first ever to use a white ball. But that wasn't the first time a New Zealand side had played at Stamford Bridge - way back in February, 1908, the game's first touring team the "All Golds" beat the best of British 18-6 in the second Test of their pioneering series. It was the first Northern Union match to be played in London.

A third Rugby League game was staged at Chelsea in 1983 when Fulham played their final game of the season against Cardiff Blue Dragons there, on the eve of the Challenge Cup Final at Wembley.

The British Empire X111 which played the New Zealanders at Stamford Bridge on 23rd January, 1952 was: JACK CUNLIFFE (Wigan); BRIAN BEVAN (Warrington), TREVOR ALLAN (Leigh), ERNEST WARD (Bradford Northern), LIONEL COOPER (Huddersfield); JACK BROOME (Wigan), ALBERT PEPPERELL (Workington Town); FRANK BARTON (Wigan), TOM McKINNEY (Salford), ALAN PRESCOTT (St.Helens), HARRY BATH (Warrington), ARTHUR CLUES (Leeds) and DAVE VALENTINE (Huddersfield).

For the record, a crowd reported as 6,800 provided receipts of £1,113 at Chelsea that night, and they saw the British Empire X111 record a 26-2 win over the Kiwis. The Empire team scored six tries, with Lionel Cooper registering a hat-trick and other touchdowns by Brian Bevan, Trevor Allan and Dave Valentine, whilst Ernest Ward kicked four goals. The New Zealanders' only reply was a penalty kicked by full-back Des White. The referee was Mr. Charlie Appleton of Warrington, one of the top officials of the time.

WHAT'S IN A NAME?

ROCKY TURNER - the iron man.

RUGBY League nicknames have a culture all of their own. Not the current trend of just adding a "y" here and (in yet more homage to the Australianisation of the British game) an "o" there - as in "Scully" or "Stevo" - but *bona-fide* names that make a kind of code-speak for long-serving followers of the game. Maybe it's an initiation test of your credentials as a Rugby League supporter in that, if you don't recognise certain names, you can't really speak the language of the game.

Other sports may have their own well known nicknames - after all, footballer Nat Lofthouse was *"The Lion of Vienna"* - but the history of Rugby League overflows with them. Some are very special in the folk-lore of the game, for example Harold Wagstaff was *"The Prince of Centres,"* a title that numerous others have been linked with subsequently, but which belongs first and foremost to the great leader in the *"Rorke's Drift"* Test (there's another name for you!). Years later, Vince Karalius became *"The Wild Bull of the Pampas,"* - and everybody knew that Eric Harris was *"The Toowoomba Ghost."* None of these were nicknames to be used in conversation with the individuals concerned, they were for the written word only to be used in the recording of great deeds like one of Arthur's Knights of the Round Table would carry his title.

The Australians managed to combine both kinds of nickname in their most famous of all, as Herbert Henry Messenger was known to everybody as "Dally" and is still celebrated to this day as *"The Master."* Years later Clive Churchill came along to be named *"The Little Master."* And whilst it seems having a nickname is a national pas-time in Australia, in Rugby League they could still manage to go the extra mile for special individuals like Keith *"Golden Boots"* Barnes.

Back home in England, Eddie Waring was the man who had a flair for showmanship and who had seen at first hand how the Aussies loved to create "designer labels" for their Rugby League stars - so it was Eddie who could take most of the credit for creating such well known tags as *"The Cornish Express"* for Graham Paul, *"The Dodger"* for Roger Millward and *"Sergeant Major"* for referee Eric Clay.

Compared to other Rugby League nations in the past like Australia and France, the British were not quite so obsessed with having nicknames, despite being set an early lead by the very first Lions tour captain "Jumbo" Lomas. But we did come to celebrate some of our stars with names that their parents had never intended. Hence, Alan Hardisty was always "Chuck," Peter Flanagan was "Flash," and Derek Turner was known as "Rocky" decades before Sylvester Stallone made his first movie.

Sometimes, it got to the point where players were so well known by their nicknames that only close family members could tell you the real names on their birth cer-tificates. Did you know that "Charlie" Stone was really called Richard or "Sammy" Lloyd was really called Geoff? In Cumberland this was commonplace, and gener-ations of even the keenest Rugby League fans might struggle to know the "proper" names of players like: "Happy" Wilson, "Tint Irving," "Boxer" Walker, "Fizzer" Dawson, "Smiler" Allen, "Pongo" Wareing, "Sol" Roper, "Eppie" Gibson, "Spanky" McFarlane, "Loppy" O'Neill or "Jazzer" Curwen.

It was the same for the Australians, all the way from "Chimpy" Busch in the pre-War days to "Sludge" Rogers or "Joey" Johns in more recent times. A selection of the best known Aussie nicknames would include: Ian Walsh "Abdul," Graeme Langlands "Chang," Johnny Raper "Chook," Max Krilich "Thrower," Bob Fulton "Bozo," Wayne Pearce "Junior," Bob O'Reilly "Bear," John O'Neill "Lurch," Craig Young "Albert," Rod Reddy "Rocket," Mal Meninga "George," Paul Vautin "Fatty," Steve Roach "Blocker," Paul Harragon "Chief," Brett Kimmorley "Noddy" - all names which the individuals concerned accepted for everyday use. But there were some good media creations as well, like Steve Ella "The Zip-zip man" and Glenn Lazarus "The Brick with eyes."

The French were just as hooked on nicknames - the best known used universally, like *"Pipette"* Puig-Aubert, *"Papillon"* Pierre Lacaze, *"Gijou"* Gilbert Benausse, *"Bison"* Andre Savonne, *"Lolo"* Louis Mazon, *"Gitan"* Raoul Perez, *"Agnat"* Robert Eramouspe, *"Le Python"* J.C.Cros or *"L'Espagnol"* Martin Martin. But they had some memorable more intricate names, including *"The Basque Sorcerer"* Felix Bergese, *"Monsieur 10,000 Voltes"* Georges Bonnet, *"Monsieur Caramel"* Christian Sabatie and *"Le Petit Prince"* Serge Marsolan.

MEMORIES

RED DEVILS IN CUMBRIA

L. MARSON (Wakefield T.) T. O'GRADY (Oldham) B. RADFORD (Bradford N.) P. DAVIES (Widnes)

I. PROCTER (Bramley) L. WILLIAMS (Hunslet) N. HARRIS (Rochdale H.) J. H. CARR (Whitehaven)

(Above) A scene from the late 1970s as Salford travelled north to play Whitehaven at the Recreation Ground. Steve Nash is the Red Devils' player being tackled by Whitehaven's David Martin and Keith Hodgson, whilst his Salford colleagues Kevin Ashcroft and Harold Henney look on.

(Right) This was how Rugby League used to present its stars - a cutting from the *"Rugby Favourites"* booklet published in 1952, showing eight of the well known players of that time.

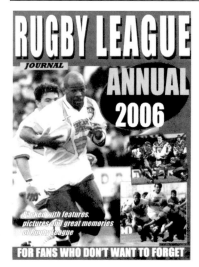

Don't miss your
"RUGBY LEAGUE JOURNAL"

(The Original Spirit of 'Open Rugby')

Published quarterly the *"Rugby League Journal"* brings you four issues per year of high quality literature. If you enjoy the nostalgia of looking back on the game you used to know, its players, teams and famous events, with every issue illustrated with a wonderful collection of old black and white photographs all printed on glossy art paper, the *"Rugby League Journal"* is for you. Mixed with analysis and comment on current affairs in the world of Rugby League from writers with vast experience in the game including former Great Britain coach Maurice Bamford and the notorious Syd Scoop, plus book reviews and obituaries, every issue of the *"Rugby League Journal"* provides a hugely enjoyable mix of history, memorabilia and comment.

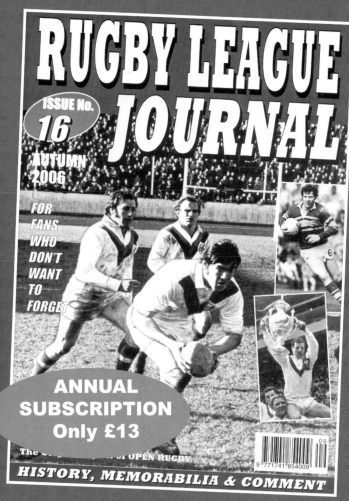

Club Nostalgia QUIZ ANSWERS

How did your memory and knowledge of Rugby League stand up to the questions on each page of our *"Club Nostalgia"* section (pages 44 to 76) of this Annual? Test yourself here with the answers.

GEOFF GUNNEY playing for Hunslet at Parkside against Doncaster.

Barrow: Willie Horne and Alan Hodkinson
Batley: Carl Gibson in 1985
Blackpool: Reg Parker
Bradford: Robbie Paul
Bramley: Arthur Keegan
Castleford: Newcastle Knights
Dewsbury: Eddie Waring
Doncaster: Les Belshaw
Featherstone: Laurie Gant
Halifax: Albert Fearnley
Harlequins: Reg Bowden and they beat Wigan

Huddersfield: Harold Wagstaff
Hull: David Topliss
Hull K.R.: Arthur Beetson
Hunslet: Geoff Gunney
Keighley: David Ellis
Leeds: Lewis Jones
Leigh: Jimmy Ledgard
Oldham: Phil Larder and Mike Ford
Rochdale: Joe Chamberlain
Salford: Brian Snape
Sheffield: Mark Aston
St.Helens: Dick Huddart

Swinton: Albert Blan
Wakefield: Berwyn Jones
Whitehaven: Aaron Lester
Warrington: Cec Mountford
Wigan: Chris Hesketh (and he played for Salford!)
Widnes: Frank Myler
Workington: Gus Risman, Jim Brough and Alan Prescott
York: Geoff Smith and Mick Sullivan

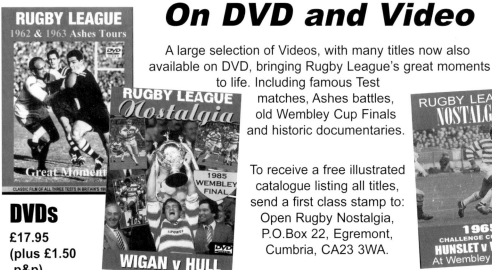

GEORGE FAIRBAIRN in 1979.

(Pictured): **DENNIS HARTLEY** in the 1970 Ashes series.

TOMMY BISHOP in 1966.

THE COMPLETE REGISTER OF BRITISH INTERNATIONALS

Here and on the following pages we present the complete register of players who have appeared for Great Britain in full Test matches and World Cup games from the first one in 1907-08 to date (i.e. up to and including the June 2006 match versus a New Zealand X111 played at St.Helens, as this book was published before the 2006 Tri-Nations matches were played.) Records do not include matches against France before 1957, the year in which Great Britain-France games were given official Test match status.

KEY: After the player's name we list his total number of Great Britain appearances in brackets with a plus sign indicating substitute appearances, e.g. (5+2); the club(s) he was with, and the years which signify the duration of his G.B. career. *The letters "R.D." indicate the thirteen men who played in the legendary "Rorke's Drift" Test in 1914.*

A

ACKERLEY, Alvin (2) Halifax: 1952-1958.
ADAMS, Les (1) Leeds: 1932.
ADAMS, Mick (11+2) Widnes: 1979-1984.

ANDERSON, Paul (+10) Bradford: 1999 - 2003
ARKWRIGHT, Chris (+2) St.Helens: 1985.
ARKWRIGHT, Jack (6) Warrington: 1936-1937.

ARMITT, Tommy (8) Swinton: 1933-1937.
ASHBY, Ray (2) Liverpool City & Wigan: 1964 - 1965.
ASHCROFT, Ernest (11) Wigan: 1947 - 1954.

ASHCROFT, Kevin (5+1) Leigh & Warrington: 1968 - 1974.
ASHTON, Eric (26) Wigan: 1957 - 1963.
ASHURST, Bill (3) Wigan: 1971 -1972.
ASKIN, Tommy (6) Featherstone Rovers: 1928.
ASPINALL, Willie (1) Warrington: 1966.
ASTON, Len (3) St.Helens: 1947.
ASTON, Mark (+1) Sheffield Eagles: 1991.
ATCHESON, Paul (2+1) St.Helens: 1997.
ATKINSON, Arthur (11) Castleford: 1929 - 1936.
ATKINSON, John (26) Leeds: 1968 - 1980.
AVERY, Bert (4) Oldham: 1910 -1911

B

BACON, Jim (11) Leeds: 1920 - 1926.
BAILEY, Ryan (+4) Leeds: 2004.
BARENDS, David (2) Bradford: 1979.
BARTON, Frank (1) Wigan: 1951.
BARTON, John (2) Wigan: 1960 - 1961.
BASNETT, John (2) Widnes: 1984 - 1986.
BASSETT, Arthur (2) Halifax: 1946.
BATEMAN, Allan (1+2) Warrington: 1992 - 1994.
BATES, Alan (2+2) Dewsbury: 1974.
BATTEN, Billy (10) Hunslet & Hull: 1907 - 1921.
BATTEN, Eric (4) Bradford: 1946 - 1947.
BATTEN, Ray (3) Leeds: 1969 - 1973.
BAXTER, Johnnie (1) Rochdale Hornets: 1907.
BEAMES, Jack (2) Halifax: 1921.
BEARDMORE, Kevin (13+1) Castleford: 1984 - 1990.
BELSHAW, Billy (8) Liverpool St. & Warrington: 1936 - 1937.
BENNETT, Jack (7) Rochdale & Wigan: 1924 - 1926.
BENTHAM, Billy (2) Broughton Rangers: 1924.
BENTHAM, Nat (10) Wigan Highfield, Halifax and
Warrington: 1928 - 1929.
BENTLEY, John (2) Leeds and Halifax: 1992 - 1994.
BENTLEY, Keith (1) Widnes: 1980.
BENYON, Billy (5+1) St.Helens: 1971 - 1972.
BETTS, Denis (30+2) Wigan & Auckland Warr.: 1990 - 1999.
BEVAN, Dai (1) Wigan: 1952.
BEVAN, John (6) Warrington: 1974 - 1978.
BEVERLEY, Harry (6) Hunslet & Halifax: 1936 - 1937.
BIBB, Chris (1) Featherstone Rovers: 1990.
BIRCH, Jim (1) Leeds: 1907.
BISHOP, David (+1) Hull K.R.: 1990.
BISHOP, Tommy (15) St.Helens: 1966 - 1969.
BLAN, Billy (3) Wigan: 1951.
BLINKHORN, Tom (1) Warrington: 1929.
BOLTON, David (23) Wigan: 1957 - 1963.
BOSTON, Billy (31) Wigan: 1954 - 1963.
BOTT, Charlie (1) Oldham: 1966.
BOWDEN, Jim (3) Huddersfield: 1954.
BOWEN, Frank (3) St.Helens Recs.: 1928.

BOWMAN, Eddie (4) Workington Town: 1977.
BOWMAN, Harold (8) Hull: 1924 - 1929.
BOWMAN, Ken (3) Huddersfield: 1962 - 1963.
BOYLEN, Frank (1) Hull: 1908.
BRADSHAW, Tommy (6) Wigan: 1947 - 1950.
BRIDGES, John "Keith" (3) Featherstone Rovers: 1974.
BRIERS, Lee (1) Warrington: 2001.
BRIGGS, Brian (1) Huddersfield: 1954
BROADBENT, Paul (8) Sheffield Eagles: 1996 - 1997.
BROGDEN, Stanley (16) Huddersfield & Leeds: 1929 - 1937.
BROOKE, Ian (13) Bradford & Wakefield: 1966 - 1968.
BROOKS, Ernest (3) Warrington: 1908.
BROUGH, Albert (2) Oldham: 1924.
BROUGH, Jim (5) Leeds: 1928 - 1936.
BROWN, Gordon (6) Leeds: 1954 - 1955.
BRYANT, Bill (4+1) Castleford: 1964 - 1967.
BUCKLEY, Alan (7) Swinton: 1963 - 1966.
BURGESS, Bill Snr. (16) Barrow: 1924 - 1929.
BURGESS, Bill Jnr. (14) Barrow: 1962 - 1969.
BURGHAM, Oliver (1) Halifax: 1911.
BURKE, Mick (14+1) Widnes: 1980 - 1986.
BURNELL, Alf (3) Hunslet: 1951 - 1954.
BURROW, Rob (+1) Leeds: 2005.
BURTON, Chris (8+1) Hull K.R.: 1982 - 1987.
BURWELL, Alan (7+1) Hull K.R.: 1967 - 1969.
BUTTERS, Fred (2) Swinton: 1929.

C

CAIRNS, David (2) Barrow: 1984.
CAMILLERI, Chris (2) Barrow: 1980.
CARLTON, Frank (2) St.Helens & Wigan: 1958 - 1962.
CARNEY, Brian (12) Wigan: 2003 - 2005.
CARR, Charlie (7) Barrow: 1924 - 1926.
CARTWRIGHT, Joe (7) Leigh: 1920 - 1921.
CASE, Brian (6+1) Wigan: 1984 - 1988.
CASEY, Len (12+2) Hull K.R. & Bradford: 1977 - 1983.
CASSIDY, Mick (1+3) Wigan: 1994 - 1997.
CASTLE, Frank (4) Barrow: 1952 - 1954.
CHALLINOR, Jim (3) Warrington: 1958 - 1960.
CHARLTON, Paul (18+1) Workington & Salford: 1965 - 1974.
CHERRINGTON, Norman (1) Wigan: 1960.
CHILCOTT, Jack (3) *R.D.* (Huddersfield): 1914.
CHISNALL, David (2) Leigh: 1970.
CHISNALL, Eric (4) St.Helens: 1974.
CLAMPITT, James (3) Broughton Rangers: 1907 - 1914.
CLARK, Douglas (11) *R.D.* Huddersfield: 1911 - 1920.

CLARK, Garry (3) Hull K.R.: 1984 - 1985.
CLARK, Mick (5) Leeds: 1968.
CLARKE, Colin (7) Wigan: 1965 - 1973.
CLARKE, Phil (15+1) Wigan: 1990 - 1994.
CLAWSON, Terry (14) Featherstone Rovers, Leeds and Oldham: 1962 - 1974.
CLOSE, Don (1) Huddersfield: 1967.
COLDRICK, Percy (4) *R.D.* Wigan: 1914.
COLLIER, Frank (2) Wigan & Widnes: 1963 - 1964.
CONNOLLY, Gary (28+3) St.Helens, Wigan and Leeds: 1991 - 2003.
CORDLE, Gerald (1) Bradford: 1990.
COULMAN, Mike (2+1) Salford: 1971.
COURTNEY, Neil (+1) Warrington: 1982.
COVERDALE, Bob (4) Hull: 1954
COWIE, Neil (3) Wigan: 1993 - 1998.
CRACKNELL, Dick (2) Huddersfield: 1951.
CRANE, Mick (1) Hull: 1982.
CREASSER, David (2+2) Leeds: 1985 - 1988.
CROOKS, Lee (17+2) Hull, Leeds & Castleford: 1982 - 1994.
CROSTON, Jim (1) Castleford: 1937
CROWTHER, Hector (1) Hunslet: 1929.
CUMMINS, Francis (3) Leeds: 1998 - 1999.
CUNLIFFE, Billy (11) Warrington: 1920 - 1926.
CUNLIFFE, Jack (4) Wigan: 1950 - 1954.
CUNNIFFE, Bernard (1) Castleford: 1937.
CUNNINGHAM, Eddie (1) St.Helens: 1978.
CUNNINGHAM, Keiron (16) St.Helens: 1996 - 2006.
CURRAN, George (6) Salford: 1946 - 1948.
CURRIER, Andy (2) Widnes: 1989 - 1993.
CURZON, Ephraim (1) Salford: 1910.

D

DAGNALL, Bob (4) St.Helens: 1961 - 1965.
DALGREEN, John (1) Fulham: 1982.
DANBY, Tom (3) Salford: 1950.
DANIELS, Arthur (3) Halifax: 1952 - 1955.
DANNATT, Andy (3) Hull: 1985 - 1991.
DARWELL, Joe (5) Leigh: 1924.
DAVIES, Alan (20) Oldham: 1955 - 1960.
DAVIES, Billy (1) Swinton: 1968.
DAVIES, Billy J. (1) Castleford: 1933.
DAVIES, Evan (3) Oldham: 1920.
DAVIES, Jim (2) Huddersfield: 1911.
DAVIES, Jonathan (12+1) Widnes & Warrington: 1990 - 1994.
DAVIES, Will T. (1) Halifax: 1911.
DAVIES, William A. (2) *R.D.* Leeds: 1914.
DAVIES, Willie T.H. (3) Bradford: 1946 - 1947.
DAWSON, Edgar (1) York: 1956.
DEACON, Paul (10+1) Bradford: 2001 - 2005.
DERMOTT, Martin (11) Wigan: 1990 - 1993.
DEVEREUX, John (6+2) Widnes: 1992 - 1993.
DICK, Kevin (2) Leeds: 1980.
DICKENSON, George (1) Warrington: 1908.
DICKINSON, Roy (2) Leeds: 1985.

DINGSDALE, Billy (3) Warrington: 1929, 1933.
DISKIN, Matt (1) Leeds: 2004.
DIVORTY, Gary (2) Hull: 1985.
DIXON, Colin (12+2) Halifax & Salford: 1968 - 1974.
DIXON, Malcolm (2) Featherstone Rovers: 1962 - 1964.
DIXON, Paul (11+4) Halifax & Leeds: 1987 - 1992.
DOCKAR, Alec (1) Hull K.R.: 1947.
DONLAN, Steve (+2) Leigh: 1984.
DRAKE, Bill (1) Hull: 1962
DRAKE, Jim (1) Hull: 1960.
DRUMMOND, Des (24) Leigh & Warrington: 1980 - 1988.
DUANE, Ronnie (3) Warrington: 1983 - 1984.
DUTTON, Ray (6) Widnes: 1970.
DWYER, Bernard (+1) Bradford: 1996.
DYL, Les (11) Leeds: 1974 - 1982.
DYSON, Frank (1) Huddersfield: 1959.

E

EASTWOOD, Paul (13) Hull: 1990 - 1992.
ECCLES, Bob (1) Warrington: 1982.
ECCLES, Percy (1) Halifax: 1907.
ECKERSLEY, David (2+2) St.Helens: 1973 - 1974.
EDGAR, Brian (11) Workington Town: 1958 - 1966.
EDWARDS, Alan (7) Salford: 1936 - 1937.
EDWARDS, Derek (3+2) Castleford: 1968 - 1971.
EDWARDS, Shaun (32+4) Wigan: 1985 - 1994.
EGAN, Joe (14) Wigan: 1946 - 1950.
ELLABY, Alf (13) St.Helens: 1928 - 1933.
ELLIS, Gareth (6+3) Wakefield Trinity & Leeds: 2003 - 2006.
ELLIS, Kevin (+1) Warrington: 1991.
ELLIS, St.John (+3) Castleford: 1991 - 1994.
ELWELL, Keith (3) Widnes: 1977 - 1980.
ENGLAND, Keith (6+5) Castleford: 1987 - 1991.
EVANS, Bryn (10) Swinton: 1926 - 1933.
EVANS, Frank (4) Swinton: 1924.
EVANS, Jack (4) Hunslet: 1951- 1952.
EVANS, Jack (3) Swinton: 1926.
EVANS, Roy (4) Wigan: 1961 - 1962.
EVANS, Steve (7+3) Featherstone & Hull: 1979 - 1982.
EYRE, Ken (1) Hunslet: 1965.
EYRES, Richard (3+6) Widnes: 1989 - 1993.

F

FAIRBAIRN, George (17) Wigan & Hull K.R.: 1977 - 1982.
FAIRBANK, Karl (10+6) Bradford: 1987 - 1994.
FAIRCLOUGH, Les (6) St.Helens: 1926 - 1929.
FARRAR, Vince (1) Hull: 1978.

FARRELL, Andrew (34) Wigan: 1993 - 2004.
FEATHERSTONE, Jimmy (6) Warrington: 1948 - 1952.
FEETHAM, Jack (8) Hull K.R. & Salford: 1929 - 1933.
FIELD, Harry (3) York: 1936.
FIELD, Norman (1) Batley: 1963.
FIELDEN, Stuart (18+3) Bradford & Wigan: 2001 - 2006.
FIELDHOUSE, John (7) Widnes & St.Helens: 1985 - 1986.
FIELDING, Keith (3) Salford: 1974 - 1977.
FILDES, Alec (15) St.Helens Recs. & St.Helens: 1926 - 1932.
FISHER, Tony (11) Bradford & Leeds: 1970 - 1978.
FLANAGAN, Peter (14) Hull K.R.: 1962 - 1970.
FLANAGAN, Terry (4) Oldham: 1983 - 1984.
FLEARY, Darren (1+1) Leeds: 1998.
FOGERTY, Terry (2+1) Halifax, Wigan & RochdaleHornets: 1966 - 1974.
FORD, Michael (+2) Castleford: 1993.
FORD, Phil (13) Wigan, Bradford & Leeds: 1985 - 1989.
FORSHAW, Mike (8+6) Bradford: 1997 - 2003.
FORSTER, Mark (2) Warrington: 1987.
FOSTER, Frank (1) Hull K.R.: 1967.
FOSTER, Peter (3) Leigh: 1955.
FOSTER, Trevor (3) Bradford: 1946 - 1948.
FOX, Deryck (10+4) Featherstone & Bradford: 1985 - 1992.
FOX, Don (1) Featherstone Rovers: 1963.
FOX, Neil (29) Wakefield Trinity: 1959 - 1969.
FOY, Des (3) Oldham: 1984 - 1985.
FOZZARD, Nick (+1) St.Helens: 2005.
FRANCIS, Bill (4) Wigan: 1967 - 1977.
FRANCIS, Roy (1) Barrow: 1947.
FRASER, Eric (16) Warrington: 1958 -1961.
FRENCH, Ray (4) Widnes: 1968.

FRODSHAM, Alf (3) St.Helens: 1928 - 1929.

G

GABBITAS, Brian (1) Hunslet: 1959.
GALLAGHER, Frank (12) Dewsbury & Batley: 1920 - 1926.
GANLEY, Bernard (3) Oldham: 1957 - 1958.
GARDINER, Danny (1) Wigan: 1965.
GARDNER, Ade (1) St.Helens: 2006.
GEE, Ken (17) Wigan: 1946 - 1951.
GEMMELL, Dick (3) Leeds & Hull: 1964 - 1969.
GIBSON, Carl (10+1) Batley & Leeds: 1985 - 1991.
GIFFORD, Harry (2) Barrow: 1908.
GILFEDDER, Laurie (5) Warrington: 1962 - 1963.
GILL, Henderson (14+1) Wigan: 1981 - 1988.
GILL, Ken (5+2) Salford: 1974 - 1977.
GILMOUR, Lee (5+5) Wigan, Bradford & St.Helens: 1998 - 2006.
GLEESON, Martin (14+1) St.Helens & Warrington: 2002 - 2006.
GOODWAY, Andy (23) Oldham & Wigan: 1983 - 1990.
GOODWIN, Dennis (5) Barrow: 1957 - 1958.
GORE, Jack (1) Salford: 1926.
GORLEY, Les (4+1) Widnes: 1980 -1982.
GORLEY, Peter (2+1) St.Helens: 1980 - 1981.
GOULDING, Bobbie (13+2) Wigan, Leeds & St.Helens: 1990 - 1997.
GOWERS, Ken (14) Swinton: 1962 - 1966.
GRAHAM, James (+1) St.Helens: 2006.
GRAY, John (5+3) Wigan: 1974.
GRAYSHON, Jeff (13) Bradford & Leeds: 1979 - 1985.
GREENALL, Doug (6) St.Helens: 1951 - 1954.

(Left) **BILL ASHURST** in action for Great Britain against France in Toulouse in 1972. Wigan star Ashurst won three Test caps before opting to go and play in Australia for Penrith. But he never played a Test against the Aussies.

(Above) the Great Britain team preparing for the first Test against Australia in the 1963 Ashes series. Left to right, *(Standing):* Paddy Armour (Physio), Jim Measures (Widnes), John Tembey (St.Helens), Ken Bowman (Huddersfield), Norman Field (Batley), Brian Tyson (Hull K.R.), Bill Sayer (Wigan), Bill Burgess (Barrow). *(Seated):* Dave Bolton (Wigan), Ken Gowers (Swinton), Vince Karalius (Widnes), Eric Ashton (Wigan) Captain, Alex Murphy (St.Helens), Neil Fox (Wakefield) and Bill Fallowfield (Coach.)

GREENALL, Johnny (1) St.Helens Recs.: 1921.
GREENHOUGH, Bobby (1) Warrington: 1960.
GREGORY, Andy (25+1) Widnes, Warrington & Wigan: 1981 - 1992.
GREGORY, Mike (19+1) Warrington: 1987 - 1990.
GRIBBIN, Vince (1) Whitehaven: 1985.
GRIFFITHS, Jonathan (1) St.Helens (1992).
GRONOW, Ben (7) Huddersfield: 1911 - 1920.
GROVES, Paul (1) St.Helens: 1987.
GRUNDY, Jack (12) Barrow: 1955 - 1957.
GUNNEY, Geoff (11) Hunslet: 1954 - 1965.
GWYNNE, Emlyn (3) Hull: 1929 - 1929.
GWYTHER, Elwyn (6) Belle Vue Rangers: 1947 - 1951.

H

HAGGERTY, Roy (2) St.Helens: 1987.
HAIGH, Bob (5+1) Wakefield & Leeds: 1968 - 1971.
HALL, Billy (4) *R.D.* Oldham: 1914.
HALL, David (2) Hull K.R.: 1984.
HALLAS, Derek (2) Leeds: 1961.
HALMSHAW, Tony (1) Halifax: 1971.
HALSALL, Hector (1) Swinton: 1929.
HAMMOND, Karle (1+1) St.Helens: 1996.
HAMPSON, Steve (11+1) Wigan: 1987 - 1992.
HANLEY, Ellery (35+1) Bradford, Wigan & Leeds: 1984 - 1993.
HARDISTY, Alan (12) Castleford: 1964 -

1970.
HARE, Ian (1) Widnes: 1967.
HARKIN, Paul (+1) Hull K.R.: 1985.
HARRIS, Iestyn (12+3) Warrington, Leeds & Bradford: 1996 - 2005.
HARRIS, Tommy (25) Hull: 1954 - 1960.
HARRISON, Fred (3) Leeds: 1911.
HARRISON, Karl (11+5) Hull & Halifax: 1990 - 1994.
HARRISON, Mick (7) Hull: 1967 - 1973.
HARTLEY, Dennis (11) Hunslet & Castleford: 1964 - 1970.
HARTLEY, Steve (3) Hull K.R.: 1980 - 1981.
HAUGHTON, Simon (+5) Wigan: 1997 - 1998.
HAY, Andy (+2) Leeds: 1999.
HAYES, Joey (1) St.Helens: 1996.
HELME, Gerry (12) Warrington: 1948 - 1954.
HEPWORTH, Keith (11) Castleford: 1967 - 1970.
HERBERT, Norman (6) Workington Town: 1961 - 1962.
HERON, David (1+1) Leeds: 1982.
HESKETH, Chris (21+2) Salford: 1970 - 1974.
HICKS, Mervyn (1) St.Helens: 1965.
HIGGINS, Fred (6) Widnes: 1950 - 1951.
HIGGINS, Harold (2) Widnes: 1937.
HIGHAM, Micky (+4) St.Helens: 2004 - 2005.
HIGSON, John (2) Hunslet: 1908.
HILL, Cliff (1) Wigan: 1966.
HILL, David (1) Wigan: 1971.
HILTON, Herman (7) Oldham: 1920 - 1921.

HILTON, Jack (4) Wigan: 1950.
HOBBS, David (10+2) Featherstone, Oldham & Bradford: 1984 - 1989.
HODGSON, David (1+1) Wigan: 2001.
HODGSON, Martin (16) Swinton: 1929 - 1937.
HOGAN, Phil (6+3) Barrow & Hull K.R.: 1977 - 1979.
HOGG, Andrew (1) Broughton Rangers: 1907.
HOLDEN, Keith (1) Warrington: 1963.
HOLDER, Billy (1) Hull: 1907.
HOLDING, Neil (4) St.Helens: 1984.
HOLDSTOCK, Roy (2) Hull K.R.: 1980.
HOLLAND, David (4) *R.D.* Oldham: 1914.
HOLLIDAY, Bill (9+1) Whitehaven & Hull K.R.: 1964 - 1967.
HOLLIDAY, Les (3) Widnes: 1991 - 1992.
HOLLINDRAKE, Terry (1) Keighley: 1955.
HOLMES, John (14+6) Leeds: 1971 - 1982.
HORNE, Richard (4+6) Hull: 2001 - 2005.
HORNE, Willie (8) Barrow: 1946 - 1952.
HORTON, Bill (14) Wakefield Trinity: 1928 - 1933.
HOWARD, Harvey (+1) Bradford: 1998.
HUDDART, Dick (16) Whitehaven & St.Helens: 1958 - 1963.
HUDSON, Barney (8) Salford: 1932 - 1937.
HUDSON, Bill (1) Wigan: 1948.
HUGHES, Eric (8) Widnes: 1978 - 1982.
HULME, David (7+1) Widnes: 1988 - 1989.
HULME, Paul (3+5) Widnes: 1988 - 1992.
HUNTE, Alan (15) St.Helens: 1992 - 1997.
HURCOMBE, Danny (8) Wigan: 1920 - 1924.
HYNES, Syd (12+1) Leeds: 1970 -1973.

I

IRVING, Bob (8+3) Oldham: 1967 - 1972.
IRWIN, Shaun (+4) Castleford: 1990.

J

JACKSON, Ken (2) Oldham: 1957.
JACKSON, Lee (17) Hull & Sheffield
Eagles : 1990 - 1994.
JACKSON, Michael (2+4) Wakefield &
Halifax: 1991 - 1993.
JACKSON, Phil (27) Barrow: 1954 - 1958.
JAMES, Neil (1) Halifax: 1986.
JARMAN, Billy (2) Leeds: 1914.
JASIEWICZ, Dick (1) Bradford: 1984.
JEANES, David (8) Wakefield & Leeds:
1971 - 1972.
JENKINS, Bert (12) Wigan: 1907 - 1914.
JENKINS, Dai (1) Hunslet: 1929.
JENKINS, Dai (1) Hunslet: 1947.
JENKINS, Emlyn (9) Salford: 1933 - 1937.
JENKINSON, Albert (2) Hunslet: 1911.
JOHNSON, Albert (4) R.D. Widnes: 1914 -
1920.
JOHNSON, Albert (6) Warrington: 1946 -
1947.
JOHNSON, Chris (1) Leigh: 1985.
JOHNSON, Paul (9+4) Wigan & Bradford:
2001 - 2005.
JOLLEY, Jim (3) Runcorn: 1907
JONES, Berwyn (3) Wakefield Trinity: 1964
- 1966.
JONES, Dai (2) Merthyr: 1907.
JONES, Ernest (4) Rochdale Hornets: 1920.
JONES, Joe (1) Barrow: 1946.
JONES, Keri (2) Wigan: 1970.
JONES, Les (1) St.Helens: 1971.
JONES, Lewis (15) Leeds: 1954 - 1957.
JONES, Mark (+1) Hull: 1992.
JORDAN, Gary (2) Featherstone Rovers:
1964 - 1967.
JOYNER, John (14+2) Castleford: 1978 -
1984.
JOYNT, Chris (19+6) St.Helens: 1993 -
2002.
JUBB, Ken (2) Leeds: 1937.
JUKES, Bill (6) Hunslet: 1908 - 1910.

K

KARALIUS, Tony (4+1) St.Helens: 1971 -
1972.
KARALIUS, Vince (12) St.Helens &
Widnes: 1958 - 1963.
KEEGAN, Arthur (9) Hull: 1966 - 1969.
KELLY, Ken (4) St.Helens & Warrington:
1972 - 1982.
KEMEL, George (2) Widnes: 1965.
KERSHAW, Herbert (2) Wakefield Trinity:
1910.
KING, Paul (1) Hull: 2001.
KINNEAR, Roy (1) Wigan: 1929.
KISS, Nicky (1) Wigan: 1985.
KITCHEN, Frank (2) Leigh: 1954.
KITCHIN, Philip (1) Whitehaven: 1965.
KITCHING, Jack (1) Bradford: 1946.
KNAPMAN, Ernest (1) Oldham: 1924.

KNOWELDEN, Bryn (1) Barrow: 1946.

L

LAUGHTON, Dale (4+1) Sheffield Eagles:
1998 - 1999.
LAUGHTON, Doug (15) Wigan & Widnes:
1970 - 1979.
LAWRENSON, Johnny (3) Wigan: 1948.
LAWS, David (1) Hull K.R.: 1986.
LEDGARD, Jim (11) Dewsbury & Leigh:
1947 - 1954.
LEDGER, Barry (2) St.Helens: 1985 - 1986.
LEWIS, Gordon (1) Leigh: 1965.
LEYTHAM, Jim (5) Wigan: 1907 - 1910.
LITTLE, Syd (10) Oldham: 1956 - 1958.
LLEWELLYN, Tom (2) Oldham: 1907.
LLOYD, Robbie (1) Halifax: 1920.
LOCKWOOD, Brian (8+1) Castleford &
Hull K.R.:1972 - 1979.
LOMAS, Jim (7) Salford & Oldham: 1908 -
1911.
LONG, Sean (7+5) St.Helens: 1997 - 2006.
LONGSTAFF, Fred (2) Huddersfield: 1914.
LONGWORTH, Bill (3) Oldham: 1908.
LOUGHLIN, Paul (14+1) St.Helens: 1988 -
1992.
LOWE, John (1) Leeds: 1932.
LOWE, Phil (12) Hull K.R.: 1970 - 1978.
LOWES, James (5) Bradford: 1997 - 2002.
LOXTON, Ken (1) Huddersfield: 1971.
LUCAS, Ian (1+1) Wigan: 1991 - 1992.
LYDON, Joe (23+7) Widnes & Wigan: 1983
- 1992.

M

McCORMICK, Stan (3) Belle Vue Rangers
& St.Helens: 1948.
McCUE, Tommy (6) Widnes: 1936 - 1946.
McCURRIE, Steve (1) Widnes: 1993.
McDERMOTT, Barrie (11+3) Wigan &
Leeds: 1994 - 2003.
McDERMOTT, Brian (4) Bradford: 1996 -
1997.
McGINTY, Billy (4) Wigan: 1992.

(Above) **ABE TERRY playing for Great
Britain in Australia on the 1958 Lions
tour - he won 11 Test caps. The number
23 in the background is Dick Huddart.**

McGUIRE, Danny (4+2) Leeds: 2004-
2006.
McINTYRE, Len (1) Oldham: 1963.
McKEATING, Vince (2) Workington Town:
1951.
McKINNEY, Tom (11) Salford, Warrington
& St.Helens: 1951 - 1957.
McNAMARA, Steve (+4) Hull & Bradford:
1992 - 1997.
McTIGUE, Brian (25) Wigan: 1958 - 1963.
MANN, Arthur (2) Bradford: 1908.
MANTLE, John (13) St.Helens: 1966 -
1973.
MARCHANT, Tony (3) Castleford: 1986.
MARTIN, Bill (1) Workington Town: 1962.
MARTYN, Mick (2) Leigh: 1958 -1959.
MATHER, Barrie-Jon (1+2) Wigan & Perth
Reds: 1994 - 1996.
MATHIAS, Roy (1) St.Helens: 1979.
MEASURES, Jim (2) Widnes: 1963.
MEDLEY, Paul (3+1) Leeds: 1987 - 1988.
MIDDLETON, Alf (1) Salford: 1929.
MILLER, Joe (1) Wigan: 1911.
MILLER, Joe "Jack" (6) Warrington: 1933
-1936.
MILLS, Jim (6) Widnes: 1974 - 1979.
MILLWARD, Roger (28+1) Castleford &
Hull K.R.:1966 - 1978.
MILNES, Alf (2) Halifax: 1920.
MOLLOY, Steve (2+2) Leeds &
Featherstone: 1993 - 1996.
MOONEY, Walter (2) Leigh: 1924.
MOORHOUSE, Stanley (2) Huddersfield:
1914.
MORGAN, Arnold (4) Featherstone Rovers:
1968.
MORGAN, Edgar (2) Hull: 1921.
MORGAN, Ron (2) Swinton: 1963.
MORIARTY, Paul (1+1) Widnes: 1991 -
1994.
MORLEY, Adrian (18+4) Leeds & Sydney
Roosters:1996- 2006.
MORLEY, Jack (2) Wigan: 1936 - 1937.
MORTIMER, Frank (2) Wakefield: 1956.
MOSES, Glyn (9) St.Helens: 1955 - 1957.
MUMBY, Keith (11) Bradford: 1982 - 1984.
MURPHY, Alex (27) St.Helens &
Warrington: 1958 - 1971.
MURPHY, Harry (1) Wakefield Trinity:
1950.
MYLER, Frank (23+1) Widnes &
St.Helens: 1960 - 1970.
MYLER, Tony (14) Widnes: 1983 - 1986.

N

NASH, Steve (24) Featherstone & Salford:
1971 - 1982.
NAUGHTON, Albert (2) Warrington: 1954.
NEWBOULD, Tommy (1) Wakefield
Trinity: 1910.
NEWLOVE, Paul (16+4) Featherstone,
Bradford & St.Helens: 1989 - 1998.
NEWTON, Terry (8+2) Leeds, Wigan &
Bradford: 1998 - 2006.
NICHOLLS, George (29) Widnes &
St.Helens: 1971 - 1979.

NICHOLSON, Bob (3) Huddersfield: 1946 - 1948.
NICKLE, Sonny (1+5) St.Helens: 1992 - 1994.
NOBLE, Brian (11) Bradford: 1982 - 1984.
NORTON, Steve (11+1) Castleford & Hull: 1974 - 1982.

O

O'CONNOR, Terry (11+2) Wigan: 1996 - 2002.
OFFIAH, Martin (33) Widnes & Wigan: 1988 - 1994.
O'GRADY,Terry (6) Oldham & Warrington: 1954 -1961.
OLIVER, Joe (4) Batley: 1928.
O'LOUGHLIN, Sean (1+3) Wigan: 2004 - 2006.
O'NEILL, Dennis (2+1) Widnes: 1971 - 1972.
O'NEILL, Mike (3) Widnes: 1982 -1983.
ORR, Danny (+2) Castleford: 2002.
OSTER, Jack (1) Oldham: 1929.
OWEN, Jim (1) St.Helens Recs.: 1921.
OWEN, Stan (1) Leigh: 1958.
OWENS, Ike (4) Leeds: 1946.

P

PADBURY, Dick (1) Runcorn: 1908.
PALIN, Harold (2) Warrington: 1947.
PARKER, Dave (2) Oldham: 1964.
PARKIN, Jonathan (17) Wakefield Trinity: 1920 - 1929.
PARR, Ken (1) Warrington: 1968.
PAWSEY, Charlie (7) Leigh: 1952 - 1954.
PEACOCK, Jamie (16+3) Bradford & Leeds: 2001 - 2006.
PEPPERELL, Albert (2) Workington Town: 1950 -1951.
PHILLIPS, Doug (4) Oldham & Belle Vue R.: 1946 - 1950.
PHILLIPS, Rowland (+1) Workington Town: 1996.
PIMBLETT, Albert (3) Warrington: 1948.
PINNER, Harry (6+1) St.Helens: 1980 - 1986.
PITCHFORD, Frank (2) Oldham: 1958 - 1962.
PITCHFORD, Steve (4) Leeds: 1977.
PLANGE, David (1) Castleford: 1988.
PLATT, Andy (21+4) St.Helens & Wigan: 1985 - 1993.
POLLARD, Charlie (1) Wakefield Trinity: 1924.
POLLARD, Ernest (2) Wakefield Trinity: 1932.
POLLARD, Roy (1) Dewsbury: 1950.
POOLE, Harry (3) Hull K.R.: 1964 - 1966.
POTTER, Ian (7+1) Wigan: 1985 - 1986.
POWELL, Daryl (23+10) Sheffield & Keighley: 1990 - 1996.
POWELL, Roy (13+6) Leeds: 1985 - 1991.
POYNTON, Harold (3) Wakefield Trinity: 1962.
PRATT, Karl (2) Leeds: 2002.
PRESCOTT, Alan (28) St.Helens: 1951 - 1958.

(Above) **MIKE SMITH playing for Great Brtiain in New Zealand on the 1979 Lions tour, during which the Hull K.R. centre won the first of his 10 caps.**

PRICE, Gary H. (+1) Wakefield Trinity: 1991.
PRICE, Jack (6) Broughton Rangers & Wigan: 1921 - 1924.
PRICE, Malcolm (2) Rochdale Hornets: 1967.
PRICE, Ray (9) Warrington: 1954 - 1957.
PRICE, Terry (1) Bradford: 1970.
PRIOR, Bernard (1) Hunslet: 1966.
PROCTOR, Wayne (+1) Hull: 1984.
PROSSER, Dai (1) Leeds: 1937.
PROSSER, Stuart (1) *R.D.* Halifax: 1914.
PRYCE, Leon (11) Bradford & St.Helens: 2001 - 2006.

R

RADLINSKI, Kris (20) Wigan: 1996 - 2003.
RAE, Johnny (1) Bradford: 1965.
RAMSDALE, Dick (8) *R.D.* Wigan: 1910 - 1914.
RAMSEY, Bill (7+1) Hunslet & Bradford: 1965 - 1974.
RATCLIFFE, Gordon (3) Wigan: 1947- 1950.
RATHBONE, Alan (4+1) Bradford: 1982 - 1985.
RAYNE, Keith (4) Leeds: 1984.
RAYNE, Kevin (1) Leeds: 1986.
RAYNOR, Gareth (1) Hull: 2005
REARDON, Stuart (5) Bradford: 2004.
REDFEARN, Alan (1) Bradford: 1979.
REDFEARN, David (6+1) Bradford: 1972 - 1974.
REES, Billo (11) Swinton: 1926 - 1929.
REES, Dai (1) Halifax: 1926.

REES, Tom (1) Oldham: 1929.
REILLY, Malcolm (9) Castleford: 1970.
RENILSON, Charlie (7+1) Halifax: 1965 - 1968.
RHODES, Austin (4) St.Helens: 1957 - 1961.
RICHARDS, Maurice (2) Salford: 1974.
RILEY, Joe (1) Halifax: 1910.
RING, Johnny (2) Wigan: 1924- 1926.
RISMAN, Bev (5) Leeds: 1968.
RISMAN, Gus (17) Salford: 1932 - 1946.
RIX, Sid (9) Oldham: 1924 -1926.
ROBERTS, Ken (10) Halifax: 1963 - 1966.
ROBINSON, Asa (3) Halifax: 1907 -1908.
ROBINSON, Dave (13) Swinton & Wigan: 1965 - 1970.
ROBINSON, Bill (2) Leigh: 1963.
ROBINSON, Don (10) Wakefield & Leeds: 1954 - 1960.
ROBINSON, Jack (2) Rochdale Hornets: 1914.
ROBINSON, Jason (12) Wigan: 1993 - 1999.
ROGERS, Johnny (7) Huddersfield 1914 - 1921.
ROSE, David (4) Leeds: 1954.
ROSE, Paul (2+3) Hull K.R. & Hull: 1974 - 1982.
ROUND, Gerry (8) Wakefield Trinity: 1959 - 1962.
RUDDICK, George (3) Broughton Rangers: 1907 - 1910.
RYAN, Bob (5) Warrington: 1950 - 1952.
RYAN, Martin (4) Wigan: 1947 - 1950.
RYDER, Ron (1) Warrington: 1952.

S

SAMPSON, Dean (+1) Castleford: 1997.
SAYER, Bill (7) Wigan: 1961 - 1963.
SCHOFIELD, Derrick (1) Halifax: 1955.
SCHOFIELD, Garry (44-2) Hull & Leeds: 1984 - 1994.
SCULTHORPE, Paul (24+2) Warrington & St.Helens: 1996 - 2006.
SEABOURNE, Barry (1) Leeds: 1970.
SENIOR, Keith (24+2) Sheffield Eagles & Leeds: 1996 - 2006.
SENIOR, Ken (2) Huddersfield: 1965 - 1967.
SHARROCK, Jim (4) Wigan: 1910 - 1911.
SHAW, Brian (5) Hunslet & Leeds: 1956 - 1961.
SHAW, Glyn (1) Widnes: 1980.
SHAW, John "Joby" (5) Halifax: 1960 - 1962.
SHELTON, Geoff (7) Hunslet: 1964 - 1966.
SHERIDAN, Ryan (3) Leeds: 1999 - 2002.
SHOEBOTTOM, Mick (10+2) Leeds: 1968 - 1971.
SHUGARS, Frank (1) Warrington: 1910.
SILCOCK, Dick (1) Wigan: 1908.
SILCOCK, Nat Snr. (12) Widnes: 1932 - 1937.
SILCOCK, Nat Jnr. (3) Wigan: 1954.
SIMMS, Barry (1) Leeds: 1962.
SINFIELD, Kevin (6+6) Leeds: 2001 - 2005.
SKELHORNE, George "Jack" (7) Warrington: 1920 - 1921.

SKERRETT, Kelvin (14+2) Bradford &
Wigan: 1989 - 1993.
SKERRETT, Trevor (10) Wakefield & Hull:
1979 - 1982.
SLOMAN, Bob (3) Oldham: 1928.
SMALES, Tommy (8) Huddersfield &
Bradford: 1962 - 1965.
SMALL, Peter (1) Castleford: 1962.
SMITH, Alan (10) Leeds: 1970 - 1973.
SMITH, Arthur (6) Oldham: 1907 - 1908.
SMITH, Bert (2) Bradford: 1926.
SMITH, Fred (9) *R.D.* Hunslet: 1910 -1914.
SMITH, Geoff (3) York: 1963 - 1964.
SMITH, Mike (10+1) Hull K.R.: 1979 -
1984.
SMITH, Peter (1+5) Featherstone Rovers:
1977 - 1984.
SMITH, Sam (4) Hunslet: 1954.
SMITH, Stanley (11) Wakefield Trinity:
1929 - 1933.
SMITH, Tony (3+2) Castleford & Wigan:
1996 - 1998.
SOUTHWARD, Ike (11) Workington &
Oldham: 1958 - 1962.
SPENCER, Jack (1) Salford: 1907.
SPRUCE, Stuart (6) Widnes & Bradford:
1993 - 1996.
STACEY, Cyril (1) Hunslet: 1920.
STEADMAN, Graham (9+1) Castleford:
1990 -1994.
STEPHENS, Gary (5) Castleford: 1979.
STEPHENSON, David (9+1) Wigan &
Leeds: 1982 - 1988.
STEPHENSON, Mike (5+1) Dewsbury:
1971 - 1972.
STEVENSON, Jeff (19) Leeds & York: 1955
- 1960.
STOCKWELL, Squire (3) Leeds: 1920 -
1921.
STONE, Billy (8) Hull: 1920 -1921.
STOPFORD, John (12) Swinton: 1961 -
1966.
STOTT, Jim (1) St.Helens: 1947.
STREET, Harry (4) Dewsbury: 1950.
SULLIVAN, Anthony (7) St.Helens: 1991 -
1999.
SULLIVAN, Clive (17) Hull: 1967 - 1973.
SULLIVAN, Jim (25) Wigan: 1924 - 1933.

(Above) JOHN FIELDHOUSE playing for
Great Britain in 1986 - he won 7 caps.

SULLIVAN, Mick (46) Huddersfield, Wigan,
St.Helens & York: 1954 - 1963.
SZYMALA, Eddie (1+1) Barrow: 1981.

T

TAIT, Alan (10+4) Widnes & Leeds: 1989 -
1993.
TAYLOR, Bob (2) Hull: 1921 -1926.
TAYLOR, Harry (3) Hull: 1907.
TEMBEY, John (2) St.Helens: 1963 - 1964.
TERRY, Abe (11) St.Helens & Leeds: 1958 -
1962.
THACKRAY, Jamie (+3) Hull: 2005.
THOMAS, Arthur "Ginger" (4) Leeds:
1926 - 1929.
THOMAS, George (1) Warrington: 1907.
THOMAS, Gwyn (9) Wigan &
Huddersfield: 1914 - 1921.
THOMAS, Johnny (8) Wigan: 1907 - 1911.
THOMAS, Les (1) Oldham: 1947.
THOMAS, Phil (1) Leeds: 1907.
THOMPSON, Cec (2) Hunslet: 1951.
THOMPSON, Jimmy (20+1) Featherstone
& Bradford: 1970 - 1978.
THOMPSON, Joe (12) Leeds: 1924 - 1932.
THORLEY, John (4) Halifax: 1954.
TOOHEY, Ted (3) Barrow: 1952.
TOPLISS, David (4) Wakefield Trinity &
Hull: 1973 - 1982.
TRAILL, Ken (8) Bradford: 1950 - 1954.
TROUP, Alec (2) Barrow: 1936.
TURNBULL, Drew (1) Leeds: 1951.
TURNER, Derek (24) Oldham & Wakefield:
1956 - 1962.
TYSON, Brian (3) Hull K.R.: 1963 - 1967.
TYSON, George (4) Oldham: 1907 - 1908.

V

VALENTINE, Dave (15) Huddersfield: 1948
- 1954.
VALENTINE, Rob (1) Huddersfield: 1967.
VINES, Don (3) Wakefield Trinity: 1959.

W

WADDELL, Hugh (5) Oldham & Leeds:
1988 - 1989.
WAGSTAFF, Harold (12) *R.D.*
Huddersfield: 1911 - 1921.
WALKER, Arnold (1) Whitehaven: 1980.
WALKER, Chev (+6) Leeds: 2004 - 2005.
WALLACE, Jim (1) St.Helens Recs.: 1926.
WALSH, Joe (1) Leigh: 1971.
WALSH, John (4+1) St.Helens: 1972.
WALTON, Doug (1) Castleford: 1965.
WANE, Shaun (2) Wigan: 1985 - 1986.
WARD, Billy (1) Leeds: 1910.
WARD, Danny (+1) Leeds: 2004.
WARD, David (12) Leeds: 1977 - 1982.
WARD, Ernest (20) Bradford: 1946 - 1952.
WARD, Johnny (4) Castleford & Salford:
1963 - 1970.
WARD, Kevin (15+2) Castleford &
St.Helens: 1984 - 1992.
WARD, Ted (3) Wigan: 1946 - 1947.

(Above) CHRIS YOUNG the Hull K.R.
winger who won five caps, which
included playing in the 1968 World Cup.

WARLOW, John (6+1) St.Helens & Widnes:
1964 - 1971.
WARWICK, Silas (2) Salford: 1907.
WATKINS, Billy (7) Salford: 1933 - 1937.
WATKINS, David (2+4) Salford: 1971 -
1974.
WATKINSON, David (12+1) Hull K.R.:
1979 - 1986.
WATSON, Cliff (29+1) St.Helens: 1963 -
1971.
WATTS, Basil (5) York: 1954 - 1955.
WEBSTER, Fred (3) Leeds: 1910.
WELLENS, Paul (12+2) St.Helens: 2001 -
2006.
WHITCOMBE, Frank (2) Bradford: 1946.
WHITE, Les (7) Hunslet: 1932 - 1933.
WHITE, Les (6) York & Wigan: 1946 -
1947.
WHITE, Tommy (3) Oldham: 1907.
WHITEHEAD, Derek (3) Warrington: 1971.
WHITELEY, Johnny (15) 1957 - 1962.
WILD, Stephen (+1) Wigan: 2004.
WILKINSON, Jack (11) Halifax &
Wakefield: 1954 - 1962.
WILLIAMS, Billy (2) Salford: 1929 - 1932.
WILLIAMS, Dickie (12) Leeds & Hunslet:
1948 - 1954.
WILLIAMS, Frank (2) *R.D.* Halifax: 1914.
WILLIAMS, Peter (1+1) Salford: 1989.
WILLICOMBE, David (3) Halifax &
Wigan: 1974.
WOOD, Alf (4) *R.D.* Oldham: 1911 - 1914.
WOODS, Harry (6) Liverpool Stanley &
Leeds: 1936 - 1937.
WOODS, Jack (1) Barrow: 1933.
WOODS, John (7+4) Leigh & Warrington:
1979 - 1987.
WOODS, Tommy (2) Rochdale Hornets:
1911.
WORRALL, Mick (3) Oldham: 1984.
WRIGHT, Darren (+1) Widnes, 1988.
WRIGHT, Joe (1) Swinton: 1932.
WRIGHT, Stuart (7) Widnes: 1977 - 1978.
WRIGLESWORTH, Geoff (5) Leeds: 1965
- 1966.

Y

YOUNG, Chris (5) Hull K.R.: 1967 - 1968.
YOUNG, Frank (1) Leeds: 1908.
YOUNG, Harold (1) Huddersfield: 1929.

The FINAL WHISTLE

TIME catches up with all of us, and as we look back on Rugby League history we are acutely aware of the great achievements made by the efforts, sacrifices and talents of others who have gone before. Looking through this Annual, and at any copy of our *"Rugby League Journal"* quarterly, we see pictures of young men in their athletic prime - smiling, laughing, joking with their team-mates, but with steely determination on their faces when they were in action on the field. They made Rugby League, the game we remember. If only they knew that we were remembering them now, so many years later, with such admiration and affection.

Sadly, since last year's Annual, the Rugby League world has said goodbye to some of its finest and best loved players of years gone by, who passed away in 2006. Several of them made their mark as internationals in some of the game's most famous moments, others recognised as loyal and talented players for their clubs. All made a major contribution to making Rugby League the game we remember and we salute them - this roll of honour includes: Steve Rogers, Bill Robinson, Peter Gronow, John Thorley, Les Williams, Ray "Ginger" Owen, Jeff Bawden, Ivor Watts, Kevin Parkhouse, Ike Southward, Keith Smith, Jimmy "Pongo" Wareing, Ken Goodall, Jack Graham, John J. McKeown, Ken Kearney, Tommy Harris, Ivor Kelland, Derek Hurt, Alan Kellett and Keith Holden. And on a more personal note, we bade sad farewell to a long-time friend and trusted associate, Don Yates - most knowledgeable Rugby League writer, grassroots enthusiast and international travelling companion.

The passing of another year also sees the end of some notable playing careers as the pages of Rugby League's story are continually turned. It seems some of the modern game's favourite big men are hanging up their boots - Paul Anderson (a part of the St.Helens double winning team of 2006), Mark Hilton (a valiant servant for both Warrington and England despite many injuries) and Terry O'Connor (a Widnes lad who came from the BARLA Youth ranks to represent Great Britain.) On the wider world front, Australian Shane Webcke bowed out as a Grand Final winner with Brisbane after being an exemplary role model in the game and in France Pascal Jampy, who represented his country for over 13 seasons and never let them down during some very difficult times.

I hope you share our recognition of their contribution to the game, as I also hope you have enjoyed our *"Rugby League Journal Annual 2007"* with all the memories and enjoyment we have tried to include. Our aim in presenting nostalgia is two-fold: firstly, to provide happy memories for those who recall the game in years gone by and, secondly, to try to help fill in some of the gaps in the younger generation's knowledge of Rugby League history. I hope we have managed to make a positive contribution on both counts.
Happy reading.
The Editor

Additional copies of this Annual can be obtained by post from the address below, price £12.95 per book (post free.) Please pay by cheque/postal order made payable to "Rugby League Journal."

RUGBY LEAGUE JOURNAL
PUBLISHING

P.O. Box 22, Egremont, Cumbria, CA23 3WA
E-mail: rugbyleague.journal@virgin.net   Telephone: 01946 814249
www.rugbyleaguejournal.net